WINNING
with LIBRARY
LEADERSHIP

Enhancing
Services
through
Connection,
Contribution,
& Collaboration

Christi A. Olson

WITH

Paula M. Singer

AMERICAN LIBRARY ASSOCIATION ■ **Chicago** ■ **2004**

While extensive effort has gone into ensuring the reliability of information appearing in this book, the publisher makes no warranty, express or implied, on the accuracy or reliability of the information, and does not assume and hereby disclaims any liability to any person for any loss or damage caused by errors or omissions in this publication.

The paper used in this publication meets the minimum requirements of American National Standard for Information Sciences—Permanence of Paper for Printed Library Materials, ANSI Z39.48-1992. ♾

Library of Congress Cataloging-in-Publication Data

Olson, Christi A.
    Winning with library leadership : enhancing services with connection, contribution, and collaboration / Christi A. Olson, with Paula M. Singer.
        p.   cm.
    Includes bibliographical references and index.
    ISBN 0-8389-0885-3 (alk. paper)
    1. Library administration. 2. Leadership. 3. Organizational change—Management. 4. Library administration—Employee participation.   I. Singer, Paula M.   II. Title.
    Z678.O45 2004
    025.1—dc22   2004009503

Printed in the United States of America

08 07 06 05 04   5 4 3 2 1

CONTENTS

FIGURES

ACKNOWLEDGMENTS

This book has been a long time in the making. I originally started working with the notion of connective and collaborative leadership about twelve years ago, when Margaret Wheatley published her landmark book *Leadership and the New Science*. It provided many of us in the field the opportunity to continue exploring alternative leadership practices that were not rooted in command and control values. Since then I have had the opportunity to work with many leaders who have shaped and influenced the ideas and practices in this book.

In the course of writing this book, I was privileged to interview library leaders—executive directors, directors, managers, technical professionals, and consultants working in public, private, and academic libraries—and other professionals who provided both inspiration and case studies for the book. In addition, they challenged the ideas and practices in ways that ultimately made this book a better product. I would like to thank Carol, Karyle, Sarah, Lynn, Irene, Myra, Jeanne, Stephan, Sue, Rebecca, and K. Sue for their invaluable contributions to this project. I created and piloted the tools in the book, and I am grateful to the Women's Leadership Program at Johns Hopkins University for giving me valuable feedback on these ideas and tools when they were in the early stages of development. I would also like to thank the members of the Public Library Association's 2002 post-conference on "What Makes a Leader?" who completed the Evolving Leadership Practices Assessment. My deep gratitude goes to my fabulous girlfriends—Dian, Paula, Morgan, Cindy, Elena, Laurie, Teri, Kirsten, Christine, Stephanie, Constance, and Lin—and the Four Paragraphs writing group for their fabulous support and friendship throughout the years. The Reis family has also been very generous in their encouragement of my writing. I want to also thank my colleagues at the Fielding Graduate Institute for giving me the grand idea that I could write a book in the first place, and then providing encouragement to do so. There are many family, friends, and colleagues at various places and times along the way who believed in me, and I thank you for sticking with me. And a deep thank you to Marlene and the editorial staff at ALA Editions for their support, enthusiasm, and patience.

The goal of this book is to bring together practical leadership tools and examples for library leaders and professionals to apply in their workplaces and communities. I encourage each of you to grow and learn about yourself as a leader and to continue to find ways of taking action that gets results, inspires people, builds good relationships, and strengthens our communities. Libraries symbolize freedom of speech and literacy for all people. They provide the backbone of knowledge generation in the twenty-first century. We honor your work and dedicate this book to library professionals around the globe.

Christi A. Olson

Well, partner, that's a hard act to follow, so I'll keep it brief. I want to thank Mike, my parents, Marc, Ezra, Cathy, and Allie for their love and support, and for being my family. I thank Christi for her friendship and colleagueship. I very much appreciate the support of the Library Consultants for graciously allowing me to join and learn from them, to Jeanne for bouncing the ball back and forth, to Laura Francisco and Lorraine Kituri of the Singer Group for everything they do, and to my fabulous clients who allow me to enter their systems and learn together. I'd especially like to thank my husband, Mike Pearlman. Without him, I'd never have been able to write this book. I appreciate his love, support, stories, and wonderful meals.

Paula M. Singer

INTRODUCTION

Winning with Library Leadership addresses current and next-generation leadership practices in libraries and library systems. The pace of Internet-driven changes in technology, combined with the growing need to focus on administrative issues such as funding and dealing with policy makers, is changing library leadership permanently. Technology as a driving force of change means that our libraries are "on" 24 hours a day and 7 days a week. Our constituents continue to hold high expectations for the rapid delivery of meaningful programs and services. We are at a point where our current library leaders are starting to retire, and without preparation this will result in a shortage of library staff and leadership talent. Market and technology trends form a picture of a customer-focused, fast-moving, networked infrastructure that is clashing with command and control, hierarchically based organizations. It is only common sense that the leadership behaviors and actions designed to optimize traditional organizations are not the same ones that are most appropriate for achieving results in today's libraries.

Our cities, towns, communities, schools, and academic institutions are going through dramatic demographic changes that have long-term implications for the ways libraries serve and provide access to constituents. This creates an environment of constant change and dynamism within our library systems and organizations. These external changes, sometimes characterized as market-driven or politically driven, are challenging our own capacities as leaders on both a personal and organization level. They also impact our internal systems, technologies, people, and processes in key ways. As a result, we find ourselves having to be more creative and focused in our use of resources in order to keep up with growth and change. It is a situation that demands new and productive ways to lead and grow our people, processes, and systems.

In our work with leaders and organizations, we have identified two major gaps in leadership behavior.

1. Many library leaders and managers want or need to act differently in response to changing markets, customer needs, and competitive pressures. Yet they have few, if any, models or resources that identify and support their desire for change and that specifically address how to lead effectively in today's networked environment. "Networked" organizations are flat structures that rely on both formal and informal relationships among employees, vendors, clients, and key stakeholders to get work done. They tend to be more open in terms of sharing critical information among team members. Library leaders need to be able to adapt their leadership approach to fit the dynamics of these networked organizations, so they can be effective at leading people and leveraging resources to meet the organization's mission and goals. Though helpful, the resources that are currently available, such as books, tools, and seminars on leading change or appropriate leadership behaviors, are not written or designed to address the unique dynamics and needs of library leaders.

2. Most of what we know about leadership is still rooted in command and control behaviors. We may have become more humane and softened our command and control behaviors, but we have yet to fundamentally readdress and view leadership skills and actions from a non-hierarchical framework.

The transition from command and control to complex networked organizations continues, even in libraries, yet many leadership practices have not kept pace. Leaders and managers rely on or fall back to traditional command and control behaviors because they lack the models and tools needed to make significant changes in their leadership skills and actions. Paradoxically, they end up reinforcing the very leadership behaviors they are trying so hard to move away from. Our experiences with public agencies, education, government, nonprofit, and other predominantly hierarchical organizations strongly suggest that command and control leadership practices persist even though leaders know they are not in alignment with the evolving market and organizational structures we work and live with today.

This book is timely because it addresses a huge gap in networked leadership practices that will only increase in importance over time. This book will discuss relevant cutting-edge leadership practices in a way that library leaders can understand and immediately apply in their workplace.

The Purpose of This Book

The primary purpose of this book is to assist library leaders who want to develop their leadership skills or take themselves to the next level in order to advance the people, processes, and systems within their organizations. A 2001 study conducted by Bryant and Poustie identified leadership, leading change, organizational awareness, relationship building, and results orientation as key library competencies (Bryant and Poustie 2001). The leadership competencies described in this book are a strong fit with the needs identified in their study. This book provides a road map, strategies, and ideas for action that enable library leaders at any level to adapt and evolve their leadership skills and behaviors. It addresses new ways to achieve results through effective leadership in the areas of library funding, budgeting, technology development, project and human resources management, and relationship management with stakeholders such as policy makers, city administrations, county governments, academic governance, and boards of directors. In addition, the book focuses on how to effectively promote team leadership through practices that involve connection, collaboration, and contribution.

Why Is This Book Important to You?

This book describes the leadership behaviors that best fit the dynamics of the networked economy and, by extension, our networked organizations. The leadership behaviors that are most effective in our networked organizations are connection, contribution, and collaboration. This book lays out a road map for how to make the leadership transition; provides tools and success stories so people and organizations can take immediate action; and links actions around key leadership principles to achieve organizational change that meets desired results.

There are several benefits to doing more connecting, contributing, and collaborating. You position yourself, your team, and the library system to respond faster to customer service needs by focusing on the real work and stop doing work that does not directly relate to your goals and objectives. This type of leadership provides greater access to people and resources because it opens up new possibilities for partnering and resource sharing. It generates excitement and vitality and inspires people to do their best work. Lastly, you can demonstrate measurable results and return on investment through project success.

Essentially, this book answers the following questions:

1. If I want or need to change my leadership skills and actions to fit the dynamics and demands of the changing workplace, what would I do differently when I come to work in the morning?
2. What do connection, contribution, and collaboration look like for myself, my team, and the organization?
3. Why are these behaviors the right ones for my organization?
4. How do I apply these skills and behaviors to solve my current workplace challenges, energize the workplace, and achieve results?

Who Needs to Read This Book?

Winning with Library Leadership is written for professionals who work in public, private, academic, government, or specialized libraries who wish to develop their leadership skills and behaviors and want a road map for action and effective results. This book fits the needs of the following professionals:

1. Executives and midlevel management librarians responsible for developing, managing, growing, and sustaining midsized to large library systems in public, county, private, and academic settings. Job titles include executive director, director, deputy director, associate or assistant director, county librarian, city librarian, university librarian, and college librarian.

2. County and city librarians in small libraries

3. Professional or specialized librarians who are responsible for developing and managing specialized libraries and resources, such as medical, law, business, and research libraries

4. First-time or entry-level library administrators who need to be prepared for advancement to higher-level leadership positions

5. Professional librarians who want to advance to the administrative side of library management. They may be branch librarians, supervisors, department heads, professional librarians, coordinators of library services, and managers of specialized libraries.

6. Executive and midlevel librarians who lead teams or groups that are still operating out of command and control behaviors and who may need to transform their leadership practices in order to keep pace with the market and technology changes occurring within their workplaces

How to Use This Book

This book focuses on how to transition leadership practices from command and control to leadership built around connection, contribution, and collaboration for today's networked organization. It assists you in developing your personal leadership practices and those of your library system through the use of real-world workplace applications, including leadership in multibranch libraries, budgeting and funding, building relationships and working with boards and other partner institutions, leveraging resources in ways that meet administrative goals, working with city and county governments, and building library support within communities.

Chapter 1 provides an overview of the changing nature of leadership in networked organizations and includes a personal leadership assessment tool to assist you in identifying your current leadership behaviors and your preferences involving connection, contribution, and collaboration.

Chapter 2 sets the context for how to practice effective leadership and manage organizational change (after all, leadership is really about doing good change work) and introduces a personal leadership change tool called the Leadership Change Cycle. This tool is used to assess, reflect, and develop a road map for personal leadership change so that we can do more connecting, contributing, and collaborating.

Chapter 3 introduces the four change principles, or what we call the "levers for change." The four change principles are used to focus our energies and actions on conducting effective change in our organizations and library systems.

Chapters 4 through 6 provide an in-depth focus on each of the key leadership attributes of connection, contribution, and collaboration. Each chapter includes success stories and examples that illustrate one of these attributes in practice.

Chapter 7 deals with how people integrate connection, contribution, and collaboration in practice. Based on information from personal interviews and feedback from workshops, this chapter shows that people consistently demonstrate a preference or tendency to practice one of the three leadership behaviors over the others. The chapter provides a framework illustrating how connection, contribution, and collaboration are integrated and aligned with your organization's vision, goals, strategies, and compensation practices. Key applications, such as project and work teams (face-to-face and virtual), personal and organizational leadership development, and coaching and consulting interventions are also discussed.

Chapters 1 through 7 also include *applications and ideas in action* to help you make changes in your own leadership skills and behaviors, and offer suggestions for implementing connection, contribution, and collaboration within your organization and library system.

Chapter 8 addresses some of the sticky problems that appear when implementing new or different leadership behaviors and actions in the workplace. It discusses the importance of starting small because a narrow focus can produce dramatic results, being careful not to introduce too much change that inadvertently disrupts your organization, and what to do when your boss is command and control and you want to work in connection and collaboration. It also outlines effective ways to deal with resistance to change.

This book is really about leadership and change. Depending on your level and experience, there are many ideas, frameworks, and applications that we hope will enable you to build and expand your own leadership toolkit. Many of you are already doing the work of leadership around connection, contribution, and collaboration. For others this may be a dramatic change from what you learned about leadership in the command and control mode. Still others among you are looking to establish your own leadership philosophy and to develop the skills and behaviors that will make you successful as a leader. Leadership is about our capacity to develop ourselves and our organizations, partner with our stakeholders, and serve our constituents in ways that promote positive relationships, create meaningful work environments, foster new leaders, and deliver high-quality, innovative programs and services that are true to our mission. This is the work of library leadership now and into the next generation.

1

Making the Transition to Next-Generation Leadership Practices

Managers do things right,
leaders do the right thing.

The goal of this chapter is to introduce two major approaches to leadership—*command and control* and *chaos and complexity* (we will refer to the latter as *complexity*)—and have you complete the Evolving Leadership Practices Assessment tool to determine where you are on the leadership spectrum from command-control to complexity. It is important to familiarize yourself with the characteristics and values associated with each leadership approach because these approaches drive and inform our behavior as leaders. It is also important to remember that both command and control and complexity are alive and well in our library organizations. The key is to recognize that we no longer have to lead our organizations using the command-control approach. The lessons of chaos and complexity allow us to lead people and apply our resources in a fundamentally different manner that is more aligned with today's library environment. When we begin to understand the ways in which these approaches affect our own leadership philosophy and values, we create the possibility for developing new skills, changing specific behaviors, and taking actions that produce desired results.

Command and Control

There are two major influences shaping the leadership landscape in the library system, across government, corporate, and nonprofit institutions. The first, command and control, is the traditional top-down, hierarchical model that has its roots in the American industrial era. It was made popular by Fredrick Taylor, who introduced scientific management as one of the first quantified management techniques in the 1920s. Scientific management was a response to the early challenges of managing the efficiency of the manufacturing plant. The human element was critical to the success of production output. So it became important to be able to measure and evaluate human efficiency as a critical measure of success. The essence of management was to monitor and control human and machine resources to create efficient and cost-effective processes and systems that maximized profit. Management specialists coined the term "command and control" to describe this type of leadership.

The metaphor for command and control is the organization as a machine. Figure 1.1 highlights the primary characteristics of command and control, what is valued in a command and control organization, and the reinforcing leadership actions that maintain the system and keep it functioning from day to day.

FIGURE 1.1 Command and Control Leadership Matrix

COMMAND AND CONTROL		
Characteristics	**System Values**	**Reinforcing Leadership Actions**
Hierarchical, top-down structure	Efficiency	Commanding
Control as organizing force	Expertness	Controlling
Predictive	Replication	Delegating or communicating downward
Organization as machine	Standardization	

You can recognize command and control by its hierarchical and top-down reporting structure. Command and control organizations and leadership rely on control as the organizing force. This means that tools, such as the budget, strategic plan, project plan, and compensation program, are used in ways that control the actions and outcomes of people and processes to meet the stated plan and objectives. When used in a command and control environment, these tools are designed to control, predict, and limit specific behaviors and outcomes. The overall goal is to design out as many variables as possible in order to minimize external and internal disruptions to the organization's plans and strategies. In a command and control environment, change is generally viewed as an unwelcome disruption to the status quo because it brings instability, newness, creativity, and unpredictability—all things that threaten the existing stability of the system.

In order to control its immediate environment and meet target goals, the organization places a high priority on efficiency, expertise, and the replication and standardization of processes and policies across the organization. For example, one goal of a web-based library circulation system is to be more efficient by handling more users with a better customer satisfaction metric in less time than a manual circulation system. Experts and specialists, whether they are technologists or circulation or reference managers, are highly valued for their expertise or in-depth knowledge. In command and control environments, if a process was successfully implemented at the main library, it is generally replicated across all locations and branches of a library system. Local issues or concerns are generally deemed less important, and are even ignored in some cases, in favor of the overriding goal to standardize across the organization. Standardization is valued because it is viewed as more efficient; it is easier to develop a uniform set of policies and procedures than to develop multiple policies on a branch-by-branch basis. Another example is the standardized ordering of materials or programs without regard to the needs and demographics of the local community, such as older adults, Russian-speaking patrons, and so on. These examples illustrate how command and control is implemented in library systems. All of this tends to reinforce the leadership actions of commanding, controlling, and communicating "down" or one way to our staff and constituents.

Let's look at a few specific examples of command and control leadership. The budget is the primary planning tool in all organizations. The budget is often developed by a few people who have organizational control of resources. Budgeting is often a closed process; key staff members outside the director's immediate staff are usually not asked for input or involved in discussions regarding priorities, goals, and the allocation of resources. The budget development process is closed until the budget is complete and final numbers are ready for distribution, often only to a very few managers outside the director's staff. Even communication about the budget is controlled and limited to key personnel. In public libraries, the budget itself is made public, but the process of developing the budget may be partially closed or limited to key staff.

Another common example of command and control leadership occurs with regard to project teams. The manager or director of a library's young adult program may know the total budget dollars for her project area, yet these budget details are not shared with team members. Team members rarely have the chance to view a detailed project budget or even make changes to the budget as the project gets under way. The project team relies on the manager for the sole knowledge and discretionary use of resources. Similarly, under the legacy of command and control, we treat the development of the strategic plan, and even library compensation and reward systems, much like the budget. The information is controlled and known by a few top-level managers while it is under development. Sometimes we control information because we believe it is more efficient; the fewer number of people involved, the less complicated and the faster a project can be developed (and this is often true). Other times we control information and resources to manage political perceptions or for personal professional gain. Whatever the motivation or intention, the values of efficiency, expertise, and replication and standardization cause us to act primarily in ways that control our staffs, processes, and systems.

In any discussion of leadership, it is important to understand and recognize the origins of our leadership styles and behaviors. The characteristics of command and control leadership are familiar to all of us who lead and work in library systems. For some leaders, command and control leadership is intentional. For others, command and control leadership is a legacy we recognize, yet not one that we would wish to perpetuate in today's increasingly complex and dynamic library environment.

Certain elements of command and control are highly valuable and even necessary because they help us to achieve our goals and get results. The problem comes when we address every situation or challenge in a commanding and controlling way and are unable to lead in a different manner when the situation demands it. We need to develop another set of tools that enables us to act in partnership, to connect and collaborate with our internal staff and external partners and constituents, so that we can bring new ways of leadership and problem solving to our libraries and the communities they serve.

Chaos and Complexity

Command and control was the dominant theory of leadership until the 1990s, when a different approach to organizational behavior began to take on increasing importance. This emerging approach, called "chaos and complexity," is now recognized as being more descriptive of our fast-paced, dynamic, networked organizations. The idea that organizations are complex systems that rely on external influences or events, such as the entry of a new competitor, to shift and change the organization was first introduced in 1992 by Margaret Wheatley in her best-selling book *Leadership and the New Science* (Wheatley 2001). Wheatley recognized that the way our organizations behave—how they change and how people network and share information in seemingly unstructured yet effective ways—mirrors the way change takes place in nature and our own biological systems.

Wheatley asserts that organizations are at their best when they operate more like chaotic or complex systems because that is actually our natural way to behave and act. The essence of management in a complex organization is to recognize external change and adapt the organization so that it can take advantage of certain changes that allow it to grow and meet its target goals. For this reason, chaotic and complex environments are also called adaptive systems. Complex systems can only survive and thrive when they are designed to be open, flexible, and responsive to external changes in their environment. If they do not adapt fast enough, they stop growing and eventually die out, only to be replaced by more flexible and adaptive systems.

For example, in the computer industry in the late 1970s and 1980s, Digital Equipment Corporation (DEC) was the market leader in mid-range computers. When personal computers first entered the market in the early 1980s, DEC ignored them because it thought that larger corporate customers would never purchase computers for their employees' desks. DEC eventually went out of business because the company never adapted its product line to include personal computers. Similarly, libraries that rely on dumb terminals and fail to upgrade their computer systems are unable to take advantage of the newer services and programs available through the Internet. Libraries that fail to offer or adapt their programs to better serve emerging demographics, such as the older population or multicultural communities, will eventually become less valuable and are more likely to be replaced by the Internet, bookstores, community organizations, and by other libraries that do innovate and remain viable and important.

The metaphor for complexity is a living or adaptive system. Figure 1.2 highlights the primary characteristics of complexity, what is valued in a complex organization, and the reinforcing leadership actions that maintain the organization and keep it functioning as a complex system.

FIGURE 1.2 Complexity Leadership Matrix

COMPLEXITY		
Characteristics	**System Values**	**Reinforcing Leadership Actions**
Flat, networked structure	Relationships	Connecting
Change as organizing force	Effectiveness	Contributing
Flexible, adaptive	Openness	Collaborating
Organization as living system	Local solutions	
	Information sharing	

One primary characteristic of a complex system is its flat, networked structure. More emphasis is placed on peer relations and informal networks of information sharing. For example, a circulation staffer can e-mail the director of technology to get information, provide customer feedback, or request services. More emphasis is placed on informal networks of communication than on formal, chain of command-type communications. Staff members are encouraged to communicate up, across, and down the organization as needed. Complex organizations are also flexible and adaptive. Change is the norm. Complex organizations expect change and therefore they organize around change. In this way change becomes the organizing force. People, processes, and technology systems are designed to be flexible so that the whole organization can respond quickly to emerging events or trends. This is in contrast to command and control systems, where change is viewed as disruptive and the organization tries to control events.

The goal of a complex organization is not to control change that is often out of our immediate or direct control, but to *be opportunistic and respond* to change. In libraries, for example, this might mean making library programs and services adaptable within their communities for their constituents. Examples of adaptability in our libraries abound. We now have coffee places in the library that serve as a central hub for social and intellectual connections. The Internet has extended the reach of libraries to more and different users. Libraries are "open" for information access 24 hours a day and 7 days a week. The library goes to hospitals, schools, day care centers, nursing homes, and community centers to serve its constituents. Libraries are very much alive and integral to the communities they serve. They are living systems.

In order to maintain their adaptability and take advantage of key changes in the environment, complex organizations encourage people to create and maintain many informal relationships. The organization is highly networked, both internally among its staff and employees and externally with its customers, constituents, partners, public officials, and stakeholders. Building and sustaining relationships is critical because it is the way an organization is able to find out what is going on within its environment. An organization needs constant information about its external environment so that it can monitor all activity and change. Complex organizations tend to be very open structures because they rely on critical information networks to get work done. Information sharing among members of an organization becomes a top priority because it allows people to respond positively to events and decisions that impact the organization. Mutual trust among staff is critical in order to create and sustain healthy relations that contribute to openness and information exchange.

For example, it is possible to create a budget through an open process. Rather than begin the conversation with only a few people in the room, an open process encourages input from all departments. Budget allocations and trade-offs can be set by the larger group or team if key priorities and strategic initiatives are communicated and shared by team members and the executive staff. Project budgets can be shared among team members and trade-off decisions made in the same way.

Complex systems place a greater emphasis on *effectiveness over efficiency*. Effectiveness means that people consider solutions that serve the stated needs of the organization's partners and constituents as a first priority. What is effective may not necessarily be efficient and vice versa. In many instances, project designs and outcomes can be both effective and efficient. Let us refer back to our example of the web-based library circulation system. As mentioned earlier, the new technology is efficient because it can handle more customers in the same amount of time, presumably at a lower cost. It is also effective because the web-based technology allows more library users and a different group of users to access library resources, reserve books, or check out articles remotely and during "off" hours. In this way the library is more effective at providing access to and reaching more of its previously underserved constituents. It is possible that there are higher costs involved in doing this, but the trade-off involved in effectively reaching more users makes it desirable to implement the new technology.

In complex organizations, local solutions are favored over replication and standardization across the system. For example, the same new young adult program that is being implemented in a San Francisco suburb will not necessarily work the same way in Phoenix or in a suburb in the Baltimore area, or even in San Francisco's central city or Chinatown. The collections process at a large central library can not always be standardized across all branches without modifications to fit the particular needs of local branch libraries. Academic libraries will have different policies for reserving articles or archiving because each specialized field, such as business, law, technology, medicine, and so on, may have different processes or systems based on the needs of its users and the operating environment. A good rule of thumb is that 70–80 percent of a process can be replicated across different branches, but the remaining 20–30 percent needs to be modified to meet local needs.

Connection, Contribution, and Collaboration

The reinforcing leadership actions that make complex systems work are *connection, contribution, and collaboration.*

Leaders working out of this framework focus their energies on connecting. *Connecting* is a critical leadership skill because connections support and make possible the relational structure that fosters information sharing and keeps the system open and working. Leaders create and sustain connections both internally among employees and externally with the community, city or county government, academic institutions, and other relevant stakeholders. Leaders also remake and even change connections based on the library's goals and strategies, priority projects, political processes, and key players, including appointed and elected officials. Leaders take actions that are situational; they take advantage of change to move and leverage the organization so that it is always positioned for growth and success. They make sure the library always has a place at the table.

The work of leaders involving *contribution* consists of linking to each employee and making explicit to them how their own work or job is tied to the success of the library's goals and strategies. In other words, each employee needs to be able to see how he or she makes an impact in the overall success of a project or the everyday running of the library. We view our human resources in terms of job functions and therefore make assumptions about what employees can and cannot do based on their formal roles. Yet people have multiple talents and gifts that are sometimes underutilized at work because they are not encouraged or allowed to work outside of their specific job duties. Identifying contribution as a key leadership focus enables people to form new and different relationships and share information across departments. It encourages creativity and often inspires excitement among employees because more of their talents are being utilized. It breaks down boundaries and fosters networking within the organization and between the library and its stakeholders and partner organizations. In other words, it helps to keep the system healthy and strong.

Collaboration is the third reinforcing action. Collaboration refers to the way we do our primary work. It is used when problems or situations are viewed as complex, new, unfamiliar, and challenging. Collaborating on projects and programs, budgets, and strategic plans creates a sense of shared understanding and interdependency among staff members. It also results in effective and creative solutions because more people are involved at the outset. Collaboration brings in more diverse perspectives and talents. Collaboration can also be slow and messy because team members have to work out differences and be willing to make trade-offs for the good of the whole team rather than one individual's needs. Leaders need to encourage collaboration because of the value it brings in implementing new programs and services and solving big and complex problems.

If library leaders are not engaging their employees and stakeholders in the work of connection, contribution, and collaboration, the organization will find it difficult to respond effectively and quickly to changes in the environment. In the following chapters we will highlight case studies, provide more in-depth examples, and review some key tools that can assist you in doing more connecting, contributing, and collaborating in the workplace.

Complex adaptive systems may be less recognizable and familiar to us than command and control ones, yet as we discussed earlier, many examples can be found in our libraries. These two approaches—command-control and chaos-complexity—are both present and active in our daily behaviors and actions. At times our teams and organizations reflect the characteristics of command and control; at other times they are highly responsive and adaptable to change. There is a natural and necessary tension between these two approaches, and leaders need to be able to navigate so that organizations can maximize the benefits of each approach. Too much of either is not healthy and can result in underperforming projects and target shortfalls. If a leader, team, or organization is overly reliant on command and control, then people will experience the organization as rigid and bureaucratic (many rules and policies that tend to delay decision making or prevent people from getting the real work done), stifling (a lack of initiative and creativity because people are afraid to take risks for fear of retribution), and out-of-date with current management and leadership practices. On the other hand, if an organization is too chaotic and reacts to all change, then people will experience it as too disruptive (not enough stability or consistency), slow moving in terms of decision making (usually characterized by an overreliance on consensus), and too diffuse in its vision or focus (deploying scarce resources on multiple or too many opportunities and initiatives). Now that we understand and recognize the differences between command-control and complexity, let us turn to our personal leadership preferences and behaviors.

Assessing Your Current Leadership Preferences

The Evolving Leadership Practices Assessment shown in figure 1.3 was developed by The Olson Group, Inc., and is a self-assessment tool that provides you with information about your leadership practices as they involve connection, contribution, and collaboration. We use the word "evolving" because it reminds us of our current leadership capacities but acknowledges that there is always more to learn for ourselves and our organizations. The Evolving Leadership Practices Assessment is designed to give you feedback on four different dimensions—awareness, emotion, personal behavior, and facilitation—as they relate to connection, contribution, and collaboration leadership. These dimensions were chosen because they are the specific ones you can use to develop and practice new leadership skills. The assessment helps people to develop leadership behaviors, skills, and actions that involve connection, contribution, and collaboration. There are no right or wrong answers in the assessment. The tool is designed to provide you with information about your own leadership practices. As such, it is not a comparative tool.

Begin the Evolving Leadership Practices Assessment by responding to the thirty-six items listed in figure 1.3. Respond to the items based on *what is most common practice* for you rather than how you feel you should respond to them. When you have completed these items, compute and record your score by following the directions in the second half of the assessment tool and completing steps A through T. You will record a score that reflects your leadership practices around three elements: (1) connection, contribution, and collaboration; (2) awareness, emotion, behavior, and facilitation; and (3) a score for evolving leadership. Once you have completed the scoring, refer to the "Scoring Summary" section that follows the assessment for an explanation and interpretation of your total score.

Key Definitions

The following definitions will assist you in answering the assessment questions.

Relationship networks are networks of connections among employees, staff, or external organizations that are primarily relational in nature. They exist to foster and promote good relations among team members. Relationship networks are in contrast to *transactional networks*, where team members primarily exchange information for the purpose of transacting business.

Power-sharing relationships are relationships among employees, staff, or external organizations wherein power is shared relatively equally among team members, and where the supervisor-subordinate relationship is not the primary means of establishing power among team members.

Growth-fostering relationships are relationships among employees, staff, or external organizations wherein team members are engaged in projects or tasks that are challenging and encourage or foster growth among team members.

Credible competencies are job or work competencies that individuals can claim as their own and that other team members recognize as credible within the context of the project, task, or job role.

Interdependencies (among team members) are situations where team members must depend upon one another and draw upon the competencies of all team members in order to succeed at the assigned task or goal.

Facilitation is to engage in facilitative behaviors, e.g., to assist or ease a process or actions. Facilitating is distinguished from other behaviors such as teaching, telling, or acting from an expert mode.

FIGURE 1.3   Evolving Leadership Practices Assessment

Please rate each of the following items by circling one of these options:

Never	Rarely	Sometimes	Usually	Always
1	2	3	4	5

1. I am pleased when team members participate in relationship networks.   1   2   3   4   5

2. I facilitate team members' shared understanding of problems.   1   2   3   4   5

3. I am glad when team members become aware of their unique competencies.   1   2   3   4   5

4. I take part in power-sharing relationships to help achieve my goals and vision.   1   2   3   4   5

5. I encourage team members to identify the competency needs for a given task.   1   2   3   4   5

6. I am glad when team members choose projects for which they have credible competencies.   1   2   3   4   5

7. I believe it is important for leaders to facilitate team members' shared understanding of problems.   1   2   3   4   5

8. I take action to support team members in developing awareness of their unique competencies.   1   2   3   4   5

9. I take action to support the development of interdependencies among team members.   1   2   3   4   5

10. I promote team members' power-sharing relationships.   1   2   3   4   5

11. I cultivate awareness of my unique competencies to help achieve my goals and vision.   1   2   3   4   5

12. I encourage team members to choose projects for which they have credible competencies.   1   2   3   4   5

13. I work toward developing shared understanding of problems to help achieve my goals and vision.   1   2   3   4   5

14. I believe it is important for leaders to facilitate the integration of team members' efforts toward desired outcomes.   1   2   3   4   5

15. I value team members' efforts toward growth-fostering relationships.   1   2   3   4   5

16. I identify the competency needs for a given task to help achieve my goals and vision.   1   2   3   4   5

17. I value team members' efforts to develop interdependencies with one another.   1   2   3   4   5

18. I select projects for which I have credible competencies to help achieve my goals and vision.   1   2   3   4   5

19. I think it is important for leaders to encourage team members to identify the competency needs for a given task.   1   2   3   4   5

20. I participate in relationship networks to help achieve my goals and vision.   1   2   3   4   5

21. I take action to support team members' growth-fostering relationships.   1   2   3   4   5

22. I integrate my efforts with those of team members to help achieve my goals and vision.   1   2   3   4   5

23. I think it is important for leaders to encourage team members to choose projects for which they have credible competencies.   1   2   3   4   5

24. I am pleased when team members develop shared understanding of problems.   1   2   3   4   5

25. I consider it important for leaders to support team members in developing awareness of their unique competencies.   1   2   3   4   5

26. I facilitate team members' relationship networks.   1   2   3   4   5

27. I consider it important for leaders to promote team members' power-sharing relationships.   1   2   3   4   5

28. I value team members' efforts in identifying the competency needs for a given task.   1   2   3   4   5

29. I cultivate interdependencies with other team members to help achieve my goals and vision.   1   2   3   4   5

30. I am pleased when members integrate their efforts toward desired outcomes.   1   2   3   4   5

31. I think it is important for leaders to support team members' growth-fostering relationships.   1   2   3   4   5

32. I believe it is important for leaders to facilitate team members' relationship networks.

33. I am glad when team members demonstrate power sharing in their relationships.   1   2   3   4   5

34. I facilitate the integration of team members' efforts toward desired outcomes.   1   2   3   4   5

35. I consider it important for leaders to support the development of interdependencies for team members.   1   2   3   4   5

36. I seek growth-fostering relationships to help achieve my goals and vision.   1   2   3   4   5

FIGURE 1.3 Evolving Leadership Practices Assessment (cont'd)

Step A First, enter ratings for these items:	Item 27 ____	Item 31 ____	Item 32 ____	Then, add ratings for items 27, 31, and 32 to determine your score for CONNECTION AWARENESS. Record it here: ____
Step B First, enter ratings for these items:	Item 1 ____	Item 15 ____	Item 33 ____	Then, add ratings for items 1, 15, and 33 to determine your score for CONNECTION EMOTION. Record it here: ____
Step C First, enter ratings for these items:	Item 4 ____	Item 20 ____	Item 36 ____	Then, add ratings for items 4, 20, and 36 to determine your score for PERSONAL CONNECTION BEHAVIORS. Record it here: ____
Step D First, enter ratings for these items:	Item 10 ____	Item 21 ____	Item 26 ____	Then, add ratings for items 10, 21, and 26 to determine your score for CONNECTION FACILITATION. Record it here: ____
Step E First, enter ratings for these items:	Item 14 ____	Item 19 ____	Item 25 ____	Then, add ratings for items 14, 19, and 25 to determine your score for CONTRIBUTION AWARENESS. Record it here: ____
Step F First, enter ratings for these items:	Item 3 ____	Item 28 ____	Item 30 ____	Then, add ratings for items 3, 28, and 30 to determine your score for CONTRIBUTION EMOTION. Record it here: ____
Step G First, enter ratings for these items:	Item 11 ____	Item 16 ____	Item 22 ____	Then, add ratings for items 11, 16, and 22 to determine your score for PERSONAL CONTRIBUTION BEHAVIORS. Record it here: ____
Step H First, enter ratings for these items:	Item 5 ____	Item 8 ____	Item 34 ____	Then, add ratings for items 5, 8, and 34 to determine your score for CONTRIBUTION FACILITATION. Record it here: ____
Step I First, enter ratings for these items:	Item 7 ____	Item 23 ____	Item 35 ____	Then, add ratings for items 7, 23, and 35 to determine your score for COLLABORATION AWARENESS. Record it here: ____
Step J First, enter ratings for these items:	Item 6 ____	Item 17 ____	Item 24 ____	Then, add ratings for items 6, 17, and 24 to determine your score for COLLABORATION EMOTION. Record it here: ____
Step K First, enter ratings for these items:	Item 13 ____	Item 18 ____	Item 29 ____	Then, add ratings for items 13, 18, and 29 to determine your score for PERSONAL COLLABORATION BEHAVIORS. Record it here: ____

Step L

First, enter ratings for these items:

Item 2	Item 9	Item 12
____	____	____

Then, add ratings for items 2, 9, and 12 to determine your score for COLLABORATION FACILITATION.

Record it here: _____

Step M

Add ratings from Steps A, B, C, and D to determine your score for CONNECTION.

Record it here: _____

Step N

Add ratings from Steps E, F, G, and H to determine your score for CONTRIBUTION.

Record it here: _____

Step O

Add ratings from Steps I, J, K, and L to determine your score for COLLABORATION.

Record it here: _____

Step P

Add ratings from Steps A, E, and I to determine your score for AWARENESS.

Record it here: _____

Step Q

Add ratings from Steps B, F, and J to determine your score for EMOTION.

Record it here: _____

Step R

Add ratings from Steps C, G, and K to determine your score for PERSONAL BEHAVIORS.

Record it here: _____

Step S

Add ratings from Steps D, H, and L to determine your score for FACILITATION.

Record it here: _____

Step T

Add ratings from Steps Q, R, and S to determine your score for EVOLVING LEADERSHIP.

Record it here: _____

Evolving Leadership Practices Assessment Scoring Summary

ASSESSING YOUR LEADERSHIP

The goal is to identify a baseline of your leadership skills in each of the three leadership practices. Remember, there are no "good or bad" connotations in your assessment score. In addition to measuring connection, collaboration, and contribution, the assessment tool takes into account four key attributes that enable effective use of the three leadership practices. The four key attributes are (1) awareness, or your understanding that connection, collaboration, and contribution are leadership choices; (2) emotion, or how you feel about using or applying the three leadership practices; (3) personal behaviors, or your actions, such as your level of participation, seeking involvement, and taking part in the three leadership practices; and (4) facilitation, or the degree to which you facilitate your own and others' involvement in each of the three leadership practices.

Depending on your total score, you will identify different strengths and areas of improvement. Each of us has a preference for one of the three leadership practices. For example, in our interviews some leaders spoke about how they used connection in all of their library projects and personal interactions. When asked about collaboration or contribution, they mentioned one or two actions in those areas yet always referred back to how they used connection. This generalization holds true if your score indicates that you prefer contribution or collaboration. Your score indicates your starting point and preferred leadership practice at this moment in your professional development. It is possible to change or increase your score as you focus on identifying your area(s) of improvement and you develop strategies and an action plan for your own leadership development.

Using the ideas in action and the worksheets throughout this book will lead to significant and positive progress in your leadership behaviors and skills. Enjoy the journey!

STRATEGIES FOR DEVELOPING YOUR LEADERSHIP

If your total score is 125 or above:

In general, you are balanced across the three leadership practices and can utilize each practice depending on the situation. We call this "situational leadership." You are able to accurately assess which practice to apply toward your goals and objectives. You tend to move between the three leadership practices with ease, having enough experience and competency to understand why one practice is the appropriate one for any given situation.

Areas of improvement include focusing on one practice area or key attribute you want to develop further. Review your assessment score and identify the key attribute or leadership practice that might require refinement. Develop one or two key strategies and actions you can take within thirty days to show improvement. Remember, these are generally refinement issues rather than fundamental changes. Check in with peers, staff, your boss, and other important people to get feedback on your progress.

If your total score is between 110 and 124:

You have a strong preference for one or two of the three leadership practices. You demonstrate competency in one or two areas and may score high in two of the four key attributes. These leadership practices are familiar (or intuitive) to you, yet you may not be able to apply each practice with as much ease or versatility as you would like. Your score also indicates you may be transitioning away from command and control leadership in significant and positive ways. You demonstrate some level of situational leadership across one or two areas. Your goal is to add to your leadership toolkit by developing competency in other areas.

Areas of improvement include focusing on one or two practice areas and one or two key attributes you want to improve. Review your assessment score and identify the key attributes or leadership practices that look like good candidates for improvement. Develop one or two key strategies and actions you can take within thirty days to show significant improvement. Do this for each identified area of improvement. Remember to be kind to yourself and focus on one area of improvement at a time. You don't need to overwhelm yourself, and those around you, with all your changes. Take it slow and work your strategy and action plan so that you see real change and improvement before moving on to your next focus area. Check in with peers, staff, your boss, and other important people to get feedback on your progress.

If your total score is between 100 and 109:

You have a strong preference for one of the three leadership practices. You demonstrate competency in one or two areas and may score high in two of the four key attributes. These leadership practices are most likely new to you. You are attracted to this type of emerging leadership and want to know more about how to improve and use these practices on a daily basis. In particular, awareness and facilitation may be current challenges for you. Your goal is to add to your leadership toolkit by developing competency in other areas.

Areas of improvement include focusing on one or two practice areas and one or two key attributes you want to improve. Review your assessment score and identify the key attributes or leadership practices that look like good candidates for improvement. Develop one or two key strategies and actions you can take within thirty days to show significant improvement. Do this for each identified area of improvement. Remember to be kind to yourself and focus on one area of improvement at a time. You don't need to overwhelm yourself, and those around you, with all your changes. Take it slow and work your strategy and action plan so that you see real change and improvement before moving on to your next focus area. Check in with peers, staff, your boss, and other important people to get feedback on your progress.

If your total score is 109 or less:

You have a preference for one of the three leadership practices. You demonstrate a capacity to engage in one or two of the key attributes. These leadership practices are very new to you. You may be in a more "technical" role in the library or an individual contributor. You may be wanting to transition from individual to manager or a new manager. You are attracted to this type of emerging leadership and want to know more about how to improve and use these leadership practices on a daily basis. In particular, behavior and facilitation may be current challenges for you. Your goal is to add to your leadership toolkit by developing competency in other areas.

Areas of improvement include focusing on one or two practice areas and one or two key attributes you want to improve. Review your assessment score and identify the key attribute or leadership practice that looks like a good candidate for improvement. Develop one or two key strategies and actions you can take within thirty days to show significant improvement. Do this for each identified area of improvement. Remember to be kind to yourself and focus on one area of improvement at a time. You don't need to overwhelm yourself, and those around you, with all your changes. Take it slow and work your strategy and action plan so that you see real change and improvement before moving on to your next focus area. Check in with peers, staff, your boss, and other important people to get feedback on your progress.

Now that you have read this chapter and completed your personal leadership assessment, here are two ideas that you can apply immediately at work.

Ideas in Action

1. Identify a key process or project in your library—budgeting, circulation, or a technology project—and determine in what ways the project has the characteristics of command and control and in what ways it has the characteristics of a complex system. List three actions you can take to change the process or project to be more open and increase information sharing among team members.

2. Based on your score from the Evolving Leadership Practices Assessment tool, review your scores on awareness, emotion, behavior, and facilitation. Choose one of these areas as your first focus area and list two things you want to do differently when you go to work tomorrow morning. For example, if you chose facilitation, list two things you will do differently to promote more facilitation in your library. Examples include adding new members to a committee or project team to make it more diverse; distributing a project budget to all team members and having an open discussion about how the team can best use and manage its resources to meet the project goals; and engaging team members in a conversation about the strategic plan and how each person can make a contribution to its overall success.

In this chapter we introduced two major leadership approaches—command and control and complexity—and described how each approach is different in terms of leadership behaviors and actions. We also learned what each approach values and the reinforcing leadership actions that make it work. Although our library systems are often a combination of both command-control and complexity, it is important to understand that leading and operating within the complexity approach is more in line with the dynamics of our networking organizations and external environment. Now that you have an understanding of these concepts and your own leadership approach, we will build on this foundation in chapter 2 and learn more about how to be effective at both personal leadership and organizational change.

2

Leadership for Change

Senior executives were good at championing change but poor at changing themselves. —Hout and Carter 1995

Craft an organization in which the positive change core is boldly alive in all strategies, processes, systems, designs and collaborations. —Cooperrider and Whitney 1999

Leadership is fundamentally about leading and doing effective change work. The goal of this chapter is to set the context for how to be a more effective leader and organize around change in our dynamic and complex library environment. We will introduce a leadership change tool that can be used to assess and reflect on your personal leadership behaviors and actions. This tool can also be used by team members and staff to assess and make changes within departmental, functional, and project teams.

Change Begins at Home

Recognizing when change occurs, learning how to take advantage of change, learning when not to overreact to change, understanding why people resist change, and doing effective change within organizations is now the primary work of leadership. Of course, this means that as leaders we have to develop and evolve appropriate behaviors, actions, and skills ourselves in order to be more effective at leading and managing this new level of complexity. As we say, change begins at home. In particular, as a leader in your organization, it is best to have a sense of why, where, how, and when you want to effect change. Change occurs at four different levels—personal, team or group, organization, and interorganization (i.e., between two different organizations, such as a library and a school district). Understanding how to work with change at each of these four levels enables you to leverage your personal and organizational energies and resources to achieve your goals.

Personal Change

The Leadership Change Cycle illustrated in figure 2.1 focuses on awareness, behaviors, skills, and actions, all primary aspects of personal change. The Leadership Change Cycle tool is used when you want to refine, modify, or change behavior, evolve existing skills or develop new skills, and take actions that are truly in alignment with your personal and organizational values and beliefs. Actions also need to be perceived as appropriate given the situation or context. The Leadership Change Cycle is one of the most effective tools for assessing and making positive change that can be applied for immediate results.

FIGURE 2.1   Leadership Change Cycle

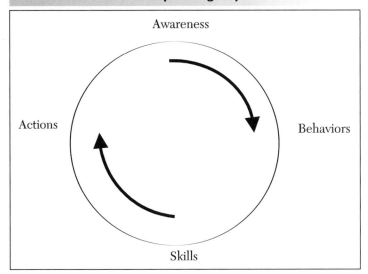

There are four elements in the cycle. Awareness refers to being conscious, knowledgeable, and well informed about oneself. In this case, we want to be conscious and knowledgeable about our own behaviors, skills, and actions. Being aware or becoming aware of your own leadership is the starting point of the Leadership Change Cycle. Behavior is how we act and react or respond to situations in different ways. Skill is the ability to do something well, usually a technique or expertise. Action is the process of doing something, an exertion of energy. Let's walk through a simple example that illustrates the relationship between awareness, behaviors, skills, and actions in the Leadership Change Cycle.

The focus in this example is on the library director. The manager of a literacy and reading program approaches her director about an idea for a new program for multilingual children. The manager speaks with her director about the possibility for a preschool reading program in a quick hallway conversation. The director responds to the idea by asking for more data and a formal proposal. She tells the manager to have a proposal on her desk at the end of the month so she can review it. Stepping through the Leadership Change Cycle, we can say the director's *behavior* is receptive (she listened to her manager present the idea) and telling or commanding (she told the manager to have a proposal ready for review at month's end). The *skills* the director relies on in this situation include assessment (she had enough information to make a preliminary decision to consider the idea and she also requested more data) and communication (she clearly communicated by telling her manager what she needed for further consideration). The director took *action* by telling the manager to put together a formal proposal for her review.

Now that you are more familiar with this tool, it is time to apply it to your own leadership situation. In practice it is recommended you go through the Leadership Change Cycle two times. The first time through the cycle, the goal is to gain awareness and be conscious of your current behaviors, skills, and actions. See figure 2.2.

FIGURE 2.2 Leadership Change Cycle—Going through the Cycle the First Time

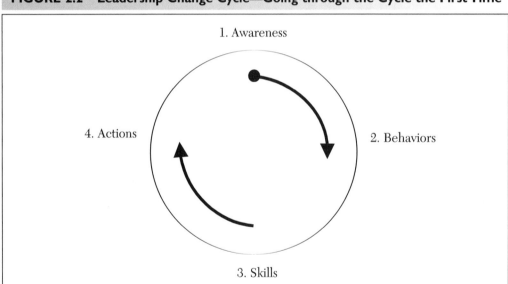

The first time through the cycle we start with step 1, awareness, and move around to behaviors, skills, and actions. You want to be aware of how you are behaving, what skills you are applying, and the actions you are taking in a given situation. In other words, you want to "track" yourself so that you have a current picture of your behavior, skill, and action. As you track yourself, you want to determine if there are other ways you can or prefer to behave, skills you want to apply, and actions you want to take that might be more effective when a similar situation or opportunity presents itself again. From there, you decide what refinements or changes you want to make for each dimension—behaviors, skills, and actions—when you face a similar situation in the future.

The second time through the cycle we start with behaviors as step 1, and then move around to skills, actions, and awareness. (See figure 2.3.) When you complete the cycle the first time, one of the outcomes is a short list of one or two things you want to change in your behaviors, skills, and actions. As you apply your desired changes, you start with the behaviors you want to reinforce and move through the cycle until you get to awareness.

FIGURE 2.3   Leadership Change Cycle—Going through the Cycle the Second Time

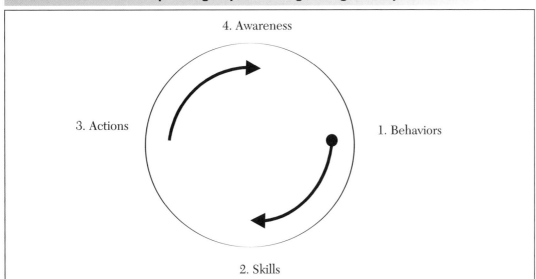

Figure 2.4 provides a template that you can use as you work through the Leadership Change Cycle.

The second time through, awareness is used as a feedback process to track the changes you made in your behaviors, skills, and actions. You can gain feedback in many ways. For example, ask other members of the team if they noticed a difference and if so, what is their response? You can approach people one on one, ask the entire team, or do both. Be sure to ask for and invite feedback honestly and openly. You will get better results if you appear truly interested in the feedback of others and are willing to listen (not talk), take it in, ask for clarification (not affirmation), and say thank you. You can then spend time yourself reflecting and deciding what action you want to take as a result of hearing the feedback.

Applying the Leadership Change Cycle

Let's go back to our earlier interaction between the manager and director and step through the cycle. As the director applied the leadership change tool, she started with awareness. Her goal during the interaction was simply to pay attention and track her behaviors, skills, and actions. Now that she has completed the cycle for the first time, we can follow her as she outlines the changes she

FIGURE 2.4 Leadership Change Cycle Worksheet

Leadership Change Cycle	First Time Through	Second Time Through
Situation		
Action		
Reflection		
Change		
Feedback		

wants to make in her behaviors. If we play the role of director, the first step we take is to reflect on the interaction and determine if our behavior and actions were appropriate. Upon further reflection, we make the decision to behave in a more connecting and inquiring way. In this scenario, we could have been encouraging by complimenting the manager on her idea or her initiative. We could have asked the manager if she wanted to set up a future meeting to discuss the proposal, or simply asked what action the manager wanted to take regarding the proposal. We could have invited her to coffee to sit and discuss the idea in more detail. Or we could have inquired as to her concerns regarding support for the new program. All of these are possibilities for behavior and action.

In this scenario we are still applying our assessment skills. We have also added relationship building as a new skill to support our connecting and inquiring behavior. In addition, our scope of possible actions is expanded by considering further discussion in an informal setting (coffee break time) and asking the manager about her ideas and suggestions for action. The manager responds enthusiastically by agreeing to get on our calendar in the next couple of weeks. The outcome now has the potential to be more open-ended because it is a mutual conversation and decision. After the conversation is over, we reflect on the interaction and are pleased that we were able to introduce new behaviors and skills that move us forward and leave both parties feeling satisfied and energized.

We successfully completed the Leadership Change Cycle by:

1. Gaining awareness and reflecting upon our behaviors, skills, and actions in the first interaction with the manager

2. Deciding the one or two key behaviors and skills we wanted to modify and add. In this scenario, we engaged in connecting and inquiring behaviors and added relationship building to our skills toolkit.

3. Taking actions based on a mutual discussion and interaction that was agreeable to both the director and the manager. In the first interaction, we assume the director's needs for action were met, yet it is not at all clear if the manager really had the opportunity to state her needs.

4. Being aware of how the change or shift in our own behaviors changed the energy and outcome of the interaction

In practice, we are usually motivated to change for the following reasons.

1. Someone we respect or highly regard gives us feedback that causes us to consider doing things differently. This can be a peer, a boss, a trusted ally outside the library organization, or a friend.

2. We hit a crisis point and recognize that continuing the same behaviors is not going to result in a successful outcome. We will be unable to meet our goals if we keep doing things the same way. In other words, we run into a brick wall and are forced to reassess the situation and our role in it.

3. An unexpected and external event occurs that is so different from what we know in our normal, day-to-day reality that we simply cannot respond in the same or known ways. This can be a crisis, such as the 9-11 attacks, or a major

shift in policy, such as a new law or state regulation, that causes fundamental changes in budgets, attitudes, and processes that affect our library system. Key employees may leave the system, or the politicians who strongly supported the library might lose an election. When these events occur, we are forced to step back, take in new data and information, and formulate a completely different response. Doing so requires changes in behavior and the application of different skills and actions.

4. We believe it is important to grow and evolve as a person and in our leadership role. We are constantly "tracking" ourselves and actively looking for ways to improve our leadership. We believe strongly in the role of leaders in leading change and know the importance of modeling behaviors and leading by example. We strive to walk our talk.

5. We are ready to move to the next level of leadership. Perhaps this involves moving from assistant director to director, from a reference specialist to the reference manager, or from a branch manager to library director. We understand that we need to develop additional behaviors and skills in these new leadership roles and so we are motivated to make specific changes that lead us to the next step on our career path.

Applications in Action

Let's work through another step-by-step application that involves leading a team. This could be an executive staff, strategic project team, or a department team meeting. In the following scenario we are in the role of director with our executive staff. We determine that we want our executive team to spend more time on strategic issues. The problem we are facing is that over time, the leadership team has become very tactical, almost to the point of micromanaging people and projects. The meetings have the feel of an operations review team instead of a senior leadership team. Our goal is to become more forward looking so that we behave and act like a strategic leadership team.

Applying the Leadership Change Cycle the First Time

1. As I track my behaviors, skills, and actions in the meeting, I ask the following questions without judgment and in my neutral voice:

   a. In what ways am I contributing to the current situation?

   b. What is the payoff for changing my behavior and the team's behavior?

   c. What is the payoff for not changing my behavior and the team's behavior?

2. I attend the next meeting and take note of my current reality.

   a. I observe that I put together an agenda that consists of 90 percent day-to-day operational issues and 10 percent strategic issues and initiatives. I realize that this drives me to behave like I am commanding others, e.g., I go around the room and ask for status updates with the goal of making command decisions. I also realize that the agenda reflects my need, and probably that of the executive team, to somehow feel that we have control over situations. We like to stay in our box and spend time on tactical issues that we have direct control over. As a team, we seem to shy away from dealing with strategic issues that are more complex and harder to solve and control.

b. The skills I regularly apply are gap analysis (identifying the gap in the project or program that needs to be addressed); problem solving, especially in the areas of resource allocation, workload, and budget; and political perceptions (I am adept at reading the political tea leaves and have a "good read" on the organization and our stakeholders).

c. The actions I regularly engage in are checking in with the rest of the team regarding project and budget status, setting up controls for tracking project status, and delegating key tasks to others.

3. During and immediately after the meeting I jot all this down on one page. I review my notes the next day and add any other details or points that I feel are important and can add to my own assessment of my current reality. I also reflect back on the questions I asked myself in step 1. I now have a better understanding of how I contribute to the situation.

4. I may even check in and ask one or all of the executive team members for feedback on my behavior. This has the added value of providing perspective on my own perceptions, since we are usually more critical of ourselves than of others. It also signals to staff members that I am committed to making personal changes and sets up the expectation for other team members to examine their own behaviors and the ways they contribute to the situation.

Applying the Leadership Change Cycle the Second Time

With the goal of becoming more forward looking and strategic, I do the following.

1. At the next meeting I revise the agenda so that the team spends 50 percent of the time on strategic issues and team relations and 50 percent on day-to-day operations. This brings up one of the rules of doing effective change work: build on the foundational work you have done by keeping some of what is working and adding to it. Be sure to stop what is not working so that you are not adding to your workload. In this case, we continue to discuss key operational issues but in a limited way.

2. We start the meeting with a discussion and dialogue on strategic issues first as a reminder that strategy is our primary goal. Staying focused on the strategic allows the team to create an early win and to build momentum for change. In other words, we create the opportunity for success. If we were to discuss operational issues first, it would be easier for the team to spend time on what they know, linger over the issues, and not have enough time to engage in the strategic challenges. This is one common way teams and individuals avoid change.

3. As director, I introduce and apply two new skills that support the new behaviors of focusing on the strategic. The first is to set up a process for creating and building the team vision and top goals. As part of creating the vision process and working at a strategic level, I realize I also need to enhance my facilitation skills. Doing more facilitation will open up our conversations and elicit more opinions and potential solutions. Concurrently, I need to call upon my problem-solving, gap analysis, and political skills because these will assist me and the team in implementing the vision and achieving our top goals.

4. The actions I take include working with the team on deciding success criteria and key metrics for achieving our vision and goals. I also continue to check in with the team, only this time it is for the purpose of trying to remove barriers and solve problems. I do not check in only to get information so that I can make command decisions. I also check in to ensure that the team's energy and resources are focused on the right work.

I am successful at making these changes for the following reasons.

1. I have a clear and compelling reason to change, e.g., the executive team needs to spend its energies and resources on strategic issues in order to achieve our top goals and stop micromanaging.

2. I focus on making one or two changes instead of trying to make five or six changes that end up diluting my focus.

3. I increase my chances for success by creating an early win because I have focused on one or two top actions that are doable in a short time frame. Having a clear and precise focus keeps me from diffusing my energy and resources by trying to do too much too quickly.

4. I am open with the team about these changes, so there are no hidden agendas.

As a final reminder, when working through the Leadership Change Cycle it is important to focus on only one or two things you want to change. Remember to be kind to yourself. You are testing and practicing new behaviors and developing new skills, so do not expect mastery the first time. The goal is to be aware and in the moment so you can apply your desired changes in a purposeful way. Stay relaxed and focused. Pay attention to how the changes feel and how others respond to you. Modify as necessary and keep moving forward in the new direction.

Ideas in Action

1. Apply the Leadership Change Cycle tool in a work situation where you want to improve, refine, or change your personal behaviors, skills, and actions. Use the examples in this chapter to guide you through the steps of the cycle. Try the cycle out in different settings, such as a staff meeting, a project team meeting, or a one-on-one conversation with a stakeholder, employee, or vendor. Find a buddy—someone to partner with—so you can bounce around ideas and get other input, feedback, and suggestions for change. This is a collaborative and

participatory action. It is important that you do not go into your office and work in isolation.

2. Apply the Leadership Change Cycle tool in a team situation. When you use the tool with a team or group, I suggest you have a skilled facilitator take your team through the steps. This can either be someone within the team who has these skills or an external consultant. Either way, you want to use a facilitator who can observe the team with a neutral stance and be perceived by team members as an impartial third party.

3

The Four Change Principles

Levers for Change

Our discussion in chapter 2 focused on personal leadership change. In this chapter we focus our attention on effective leadership change in our organizations and library systems. The four change principles act as primary leverage points for implementing effective organizational change. "Leverage" is defined as the power to accomplish a purpose through action. The change principles act as powerful tools for change because they challenge us to look at underlying assumptions that come from the more traditional command and control model of leadership. Each of the change principles addresses a key assumption about leading change that is different in today's complex, connected workplace. Figure 3.1 identifies the four principles and illustrates the differences in leadership between complexity and command and control.

FIGURE 3.1   The Four Change Principles

Change Principle	Complexity	Command and Control
Principle 1	Organizing around change	Organizing around control
Principle 2	Doing the work that needs to be done	Doing the work specified by job function
Principle 3	Relying on the group as the primary unit of work	Relying on the individual hero as the unit of work
Principle 4	Sharing information	Controlling information

These four change principles are simple to work with yet have a powerful impact when applied across an organization. They are powerful because applying each principle has an immediate effect on people's behavior and actions. Remember, when we are leading change we are really doing the leadership work of changing behaviors that lead to positive action and desired results. Applying these four change principles throughout your organization will enable you to create positive conditions for change and achieve high-impact results.

Again, we do not necessarily want to abandon command and control leadership altogether. But it is important to recognize that the change principles that match our complex workplaces are a better fit with our employees and constituencies in today's library systems than those that match command and control. Learn how to use these new principles and take advantage of their potential for positive organizational change. Let's define each of the four principles in more detail and look at how you can apply them in your library system.

Principle One: Organizing around Change

Do you go to work each day with the attitude that there is so much change going on in your organization that you feel you want to control events and people in order to gain some semblance of control over the situation? Or do you go to work each day with the attitude that all this change, though highly disruptive at times, can also create new opportunities for the library, including yourself, your staff, and the public? Our personal and organizational response to disruption and change is often a mixture of these two attitudes. Organizing around change means that we start each day with the understanding that there will always be events that occur outside of our control. Most of us know this intellectually. Of course, we say, events occur all the time that we have no control over. But in our behavior we often try to compensate by finding ways to control our environment as a way to reduce our anxieties, fears, frustration, or just plain exhaustion. The notion behind "organizing around change" is to set up some positive behaviors that we can begin to use in order to lead and operate within a broader range of change and complexity. Rather than trying to limit or control the impact of change, let us look at ways to become more accepting of change and use it to accomplish our goals and objectives.

Action Building

The following are the primary actions we want to take to successfully organize around change in our libraries.

1. Create an environment of open communications and information sharing. In chapter 2 we discussed how open communications and information sharing are key attributes of a healthy, functioning, complex organization. You can never overcommunicate and overshare information. As a leader, create an environment that fosters the attributes of openness. By doing so you will gain trust and credibility throughout the organization.

2. Expect and encourage employees to make good mistakes, even reward them. Recognize that people will be taking more risks and operating out of their comfort zone. Make sure you are making good mistakes—mistakes that the organization can learn from—so that you build organizational capacity around new core competencies.

3. Establish key outcomes or top-level goals and objectives that guide people's actions. If we are all organizing around change, and there is a lot of change to deal with, you will have a higher chance of success if you can establish two or three clear and understandable goals that focus people and drive their actions. Otherwise, we all tend to get overwhelmed by too much change. Focus the organization and your human resources on the right set of changes. It will save you time and keep people moving in a positive direction.

4. Be prepared to change directions; if one path is blocked, look for another to open. Organizing around change is like sailing. You have to do a lot of tacking or moving from side to side with the wind as a way to make forward progress. Learn to read the wind and follow it because it will eventually get you where you want to go. In this era of dynamic change, it is not possible to move unhindered in a straight line toward your goals. Set out a top-level goal or objective, and then be flexible and opportunistic in terms of its implementation.

5. Focus on the process once you have set the outcomes. The art of creating effective and sustainable change means that you pay attention to process and take advantage of small opportunities to create larger-scale change. It is in the process that opportunities for change occur. This is closely linked to the previous action involving flexible and opportunistic implementation.

6. Pay attention to the pace of change. Learn to identify the key changes you really want or need to respond to, because not all change is necessarily good for an organization. Develop a sense of discipline about how fast or how slow people and projects can and need to move toward their goals. Too much change too fast can cause people and organizations to oscillate or spin out because people are pressed to get things done too quickly and do not have time to recuperate. They are stretched too thin. Be sure to consider the issue of pace when leading change efforts. It's good to have a sense of urgency on some actions. Be sure to clearly convey why a goal is urgent and why people need to be concerned about this issue. If your staff and employees seem to lack any sense of urgency about key goals and objectives, then it is time to pick up the pace and ignite a few fires. The number one rule for leading change is to create a sense of urgency (Kotter 1996). Learn to create a sense of urgency around the desired change and choose your change efforts wisely so that you can establish a successful track record for effective change.

Tools for Organizing around Change

The key to organizing around change is to find out what changes are happening, both locally and globally; how fast these changes are occurring; where change is occurring; and why and how it might affect your library organization. It is also important to set up and sustain processes that will allow you and the organization to be as flexible as possible when you respond to change. You are in a good position to respond to change if your organization can be flexible and fluid instead of rigid and can embrace rather than resist change.

You can apply the following tools in ways that enable you to monitor your external environment.

1. Environmental assessments are ways to monitor external trends and events and to assess opportunities. Chief among them is a SWOT analysis, which is used to identify your library's *strengths* and *weaknesses*, the market *opportunities*, and competitive or other *threats* to your market success). Other tools include analyst reports on trend information such as demographics and lifestyles, population shifts, birthrates, immigration, and other key socioeconomic indicators. Government reports are also a good source of information, especially in regard to growth and planning, housing, environmental impact, aging, and so on. The goal of any external assessment is to look at the macro indicators; assess how they might impact the local, regional, national, and global landscape; and then develop a strategic plan that takes into consideration the impact of these macro changes on the library and the community it serves. You can use the SWOT Analysis Worksheet in figure 3.2 to do a SWOT analysis. You can also refer to *The New Planning for Results* (Nelson 2001) for valuable instructions on how to identify future possibilities and to *Library Networks in the New Millennium: Top Ten Trends* (Laughlin 2000) for information on future trends that might impact the growth and evolution of libraries.

2. Processes that facilitate constant and regular communications and act as avenues for people to provide input and share outputs are very helpful. Processes are most effective when they are established to promote communications among staff, between staff and the public, senior leadership and the board, senior leadership and city government, and senior leadership and library donors. Examples of effective processes include staff meetings, public forums, networking events, focus groups, information sessions, symposiums, conferences, and event fairs. The primary message here is to get out and into the community often. Be sure to systematically set up and encourage processes that result in constant and informative communications. If you do this you will know that your actions are informed by current information and input from your constituents.

3. Processes and tools that are designed to help you create and assess organizational outcomes and measure results are also useful. These include establishing a vision, developing key goals and objectives, aligning goals with resources, setting organizational and team priorities, creating success criteria, and focusing on a few key metrics that provide feedback on how you are doing. If you are able to assess the impact of change throughout your organization, then you can be more confident in taking the right set of actions to achieve desired results. If you can't "measure it" then it is difficult to know if you are being effective and successful. Use the Vision Road Map Worksheet in figure 3.3 to create a vision and establish a road map for moving from the current reality to the future vision.

FIGURE 3.2   SWOT Analysis

The SWOT analysis is generally used in the planning process for the library (or any organization). It is a tool that assists the organization in assessing its overall market position relative to its constituents, customers, and competitors. Use the key questions listed under each category as a guideline to (a) assess your library's overall market position and (b) develop a short- and long-term response to both the weaknesses and opportunities that arise as you go through the process. The outcomes from the SWOT analysis can be used as key inputs for the long-range planning process to develop key strategic goals and initiatives.

The SWOT analysis can be applied at different levels within an organization, such as the executive staff or board, a project team, or a department unit within the library.

Strengths

Key Questions:

1. What are the core strengths or core competencies in your library or library system? Consider people, talent, processes, systems, infrastructure, technology, geography, partnerships, and so on.

2. What unique strengths does your library have that your competitors do not?

Weaknesses

Key Questions:

1. What are the weaknesses or areas that you feel need development in your library? Again, consider people, talent, processes, systems, infrastructure, technology, geography, partnerships, and so on.

2. What and where are your library's weaknesses relative to those of your competitors?

Opportunities

Key Questions:

1. What are the opportunities for increasing your library's presence in the community or creating more value within the community for your library? Again, consider people, talent, processes, systems, infrastructure, technology, geography, partnerships, and so on.

2. What new programs can you deliver that are needed and valued by the community and can add to the core competencies of the library?

3. What major trends are out there that you can leverage to create opportunities for the library?

4. What are your competitors not doing and what could you be doing to create opportunities?

Threats

Key Questions:

1. What new or future processes, technologies, policies, demographic trends, and so on pose a threat to the growth of your library?

2. What internal "blind spots," patterns, and behaviors post an internal threat to your desire and need to grow the library? Examples include a slow pace of decision making, a low threshold for taking risks, distrust of "external" partners and therefore few productive partnerships, lack of focus, and lack of a compelling vision.

SWOT Analysis Worksheet

	Organizational Level	Project / Department Level
Strengths		
Weaknesses		

SWOT Analysis Worksheet (cont'd)

	Organizational Level	Project/Department Level
Opportunities		
Threats		

FIGURE 3.3 Vision Road Map Worksheet

A *vision* is a *picture of the future* with some good organizational reasons why people would want to create that future (Kotter 1996). An effective vision is:

> *imaginable:* it conveys a picture of the future
>
> *desirable:* it appeals to long-term interests
>
> *feasible:* it has realistic, attainable goals
>
> *focused:* it is clear enough to provide guidance
>
> *flexible:* it is general enough to allow individual initiative and alternative responses in light of changing conditions
>
> *communicable:* it is easy to communicate; it can be explained in under five minutes

There are three compelling reasons for having a vision:

1. It clarifies general direction and simplifies lots of details.
2. It motivates people to take action in the right direction.
3. It coordinates the actions of many people in fast and even efficient ways.

Mission describes the *purpose* of the organization, *why it exists and who it serves.*

The Process for Creating a Vision

1. Take approximately thirty minutes with a group or team and jot down (on an easel sheet) what's working for the group or organization, and what you want to change (or what is not working). The goal of step 1 is to gather everyone's input regarding the collective "current reality" so that you have a starting point or baseline for building the vision.

2. Give everyone a blank piece of paper and drawing materials (magic markers, felt pens, crayons). Ask each person to take fifteen minutes and visually represent their vision for the group, project, or organization.

3. After everyone has completed drawing their vision, ask each person to take between two and five minutes to describe his or her vision. Have a facilitator jot down the key points on flip charts. Go around the room so that everyone has the chance to speak and voice their vision.

4. Next give the group time to read through all the flip charts. Ask for clarification or questions at this time.

5. Then begin to combine similar or like points, ideas, and concepts. Continue through this process until all of the key points have either been grouped into a single idea or concept or stand alone as separate ideas.

6. At the end of step 5, you will have left on the easel sheet a list of the top five or six elements for the overall vision. From there, combine the top vision elements into a draft statement or sentence. The goal is to capture 80 percent of what is important to everyone. Ask for agreement or changes. Once everyone has agreed, assign a small team the task of refining the statement and completing the vision. Be sure to have the team review the final vision statement.

7. You can usually do this in about four hours or half a day with a group of 25 to 50 people. If there are more people, it will take longer.

8. Once you have completed the vision, the next step is to build a road map for how you are going to transition from the "current reality" to the "future vision." Road maps are typically developed like a long-range plan or project timeline. Start by breaking up the timeline into key phases—3, 6, 9, or 12 months in length, depending on the task involved. Be sure to set your top two or three goals for each phase, and list the key tasks or objectives to support the goals. Do this for each major phase of the road map. In addition, develop two or three key success criteria for each phase so that you know where you are successful and where you need to do more work.

9. Be sure to schedule a series of planning days and times to work through the road map or implementation plan. Make sure everyone who developed the vision is involved in developing the road map. Make it an open process. If everyone participates and agrees up front, there will be less resistance and more motivation to work toward the vision. This is what we mean when we say "go slow to go fast." Take time to do this critical up-front work and you can accelerate the project once everyone has a common understanding and is in agreement at the start of the change project.

Assess Your Library's Capacity for Organizing around Change

Start by doing a quick assessment of your library's competencies in this area. Where in the library do you do a good job of organizing around change? Is there a current project or work group where dealing with constant change is a key ingredient for the group's success? Where in the library system are the processes most flexible and fluid? Have you done any type of environmental assessment in the last six months? Have you started a major project—such as enhancing web services, expanding a children's reading program, or adding multicultural materials to your collections—where group members have developed a project vision, set clear goals, and developed measurable outcomes or success criteria? In staff meetings do you routinely discuss the effectiveness of your communications?

Another way to assess your capacity for organizing around change is to look at where you are organized around control rather than change. Where are your processes more rigid and designed to control change? How long has it been since you did any type of customer survey or a SWOT analysis? How often do you talk about your communications processes at staff meetings or employee forums? Are your project teams or groups set up to respond quickly and effectively to midcourse corrections and changes? These are all opportunities to take leadership and apply the first change principle throughout the organization.

We use the following set of questions to assess an organization's capacity for organizing around change as opposed to organizing around control.

1. Do project teams have clear goals and objectives that serve the purpose of guiding team members in the face of constant change? Are these goals updated or revisited on a regular basis? Revisiting key goals and objectives every ninety days is a good rule of thumb.

2. Is there an agreed-upon check-in process between senior management and staff to discuss current events and their impact on the library, both short-term and long-term? Look for operational processes like town hall meetings, open forums, e-mail updates, or management meetings that have as an agenda topic a discussion of current happenings.

3. Who in the organization has a sense of urgency about a particular issue and why? If you find urgency, then there is hope for change. If no one has a sense of urgency, then a big red light ought to start flashing in front of you. Find the rationale for change, communicate it extensively throughout the organization, and get everyone on board.

4. Are there places where employees, customers, and constituents can provide input about issues and events that affect the library? Here we want to ensure that there is some systematic process for getting external information into the internal system. We always look for mechanisms like electronic forums, chat sessions, help desks, analyst reports on trends, or anything else that would ensure that the library system is open and receiving valuable information about its external environment and customers.

Principle Two: Doing the Work That Needs to Be Done

When you look at the top goals and objectives of your organization and match them up with the people and money available, is there alignment? Are the top strategic initiatives staffed with the right people who can get the work done? Do you allocate project resources and create project membership based on people's formal or informal job roles and functions? Are you willing to reorganize project resources based on the work that really needs to get done, even if it means having people do other work or tasks that are outside their formal job function? Doing the work that needs to be done means that library employees and leaders are willing to align and realign people's talents that best fit the project at hand. In this way, the whole system is able to make the best use of people's talents on a project-by-project basis, thus leveraging all the resources within the organization to achieve success.

Laughlin (2000) writes that restructuring work is one of the top ten trends for library networks in the new millennium. The ability and willingness of a leader to assess and reorganize all the available resources around the work that needs to be done at any given time gives that leader tremendous leverage to get the job done. Doing the work that needs to be done is about jumping outside the box of prescribed job functions and asking people to work on projects based on their talents and capacity to work effectively on a particular project, even if it is not in their formal job description. Oftentimes formal job descriptions are outdated and impractical because they are built around older processes and systems. Even a job description that is one or two years old can be outdated due to the high degree of change in the system. This puts leaders and organizations at risk if they are not able to call on people to make a contribution to the organization based on need because the formal job function might prohibit a person from working on a specific project.

The ability to rethink and reconsider how we apply resources is especially critical because we are always operating under resource constraints that limit what we can accomplish at work. Library systems are under pressure to restructure work to meet the changing needs of their customers while managing changes in funding levels and policy (Laughlin 2000). At its root, doing the work that needs to be done is really about using all available resources—people, systems, and processes—for creative problem solving. Decisions about resources and individuals' contributions are based on need and talent at any given time. This principle has the most dramatic impact on an organization of the four change principles. It enables leaders and libraries to achieve success because the organization's talents and resources are 100 percent focused on the right set of actions.

Action Building

The following are the primary actions we want to take to successfully do the work that needs to be done in an organization.

1. Identify, assess, and organize people around the library's top priorities or the critical work that needs to get done. In most instances, this means using

people in different roles on a per project basis, shifting or rotating people on and off projects, and even assigning or asking people to commit to a two- or three-year position based on need. This type of project-based work is usually overlaid on an employee's routine or maintenance-type job functions. For example, a collections manager's primary role is to manage and monitor the library's collections, including its titles, media, reference works, and so on. This is her primary job function. However, she may have specific talents in the areas of strategy and multicultural environments. In this case, we want to leverage her talents in areas outside collections when needed rather than limit ourselves by assuming she can't make a significant contribution outside of her formal job role.

2. Use the top goals and priorities to influence and change job descriptions. Don't be satisfied with allowing job descriptions to define the organization's goals and priorities or limit activities because "it isn't in the job description" or "we don't have a job description for that." Even in union or government environments, it is possible to rethink and rewrite job descriptions if it is done through an open process with honest and mutual conversation.

3. Evaluate job performance based on achieving the organization's goals and priorities and not solely on doing the job described in the job function. Enhance the job description to include the organization's top goals and priorities so that it is current and truly reflects the organization's expectations of each employee.

4. Be prepared to adjust or modify the library compensation and reward system so that employees who work outside of their formal job role have incentives to do so and are rewarded for making a contribution. Flexible compensation and reward incentives are absolutely critical for success.

Tools for Doing the Work That Needs to Be Done

The key to success for this change principle is to align resources dynamically to match the work at hand and to do so in a way that is explicit and bounded by time and project scope. It is important for people to know there is a "start and stop" to a project so that they can have a sense of accomplishment and know the extent and scope of their commitment and contribution. Equally important is the ability to manage this type of revolving project work at the larger organizational level in order to insure that the right people are on the right projects at the right time. Leaders need to work with employees to pace the projects, establish priorities, make appropriate trade-offs, and provide higher-level guidelines and goals for project group leaders and members.

You can apply the following tools in ways that enable you to align people's talents with the immediate work that needs to be done.

1. Provide a clear and compelling vision with a set of agreed-upon goals and objectives, along with outcomes and success criteria, in order to guide people's behaviors and actions. People are more motivated and willing to contribute their talents and time if they have a clear understanding of what they are being asked to do and why it will make a difference. Doing change is hard work, so we like

to know what we are working for and why. Creating a clear and compelling vision is a key success factor when leading change (Kotter 1996). The vision addresses the questions "When we meet these goals and objectives, what will our world be like, look like, or feel like?" and "How will it be different from today?" Top-level goals and objectives have to be in place because they serve as the rationale for change and for all subsequent actions. Develop three to five outcomes that describe the end result in order to anchor the goals and objectives in reality. People need to know what success looks like so they can feel comfortable about doing the work that needs to be done.

2. Maintain up-to-date and dynamic job descriptions. Review job descriptions at least once a year and test them for reality and relevancy. Be sure that employees receive credit and recognition for work they are doing that fits with the organization's top goals, even if it is not in their current job description. Put together a letter of agreement so that both the employee and the organization have a clear understanding of what is expected in terms of time commitment, scope of work, and any extra compensation. A good reference book for how to construct flexible compensation and reward systems is *Developing a Compensation Plan for Your Library* by Paula Singer (2002).

3. Your human resources department should act as a partner and not as an inhibitor to change. Be sure to involve the department whenever possible. It is important that human resources act as a key partner in leading change and assist in moving the library forward. Human resources needs to be in unison with the library's top goals and objectives. If necessary, challenge your human resources department to be creative when it comes to project assignments and compensation.

4. Labor and employment unions can act as partners for change. Collective bargaining agreements need to be flexible and support the alignment of resources required to get the work done. Like human resources, organized labor is a critical partner in making this work effectively. The goal is not to have employees do more work but to have the flexibility to ask people to make a contribution based on a combination of their talents, formal job functions, and the needs of the organization.

5. Have the courage to make changes based on doing the work that needs to get done. It can be very difficult for leaders to implement this principle because we encounter resistance to change. Many people in organizations like the status quo and have no desire to do more work than is outlined by their job description. Others, especially the champions of change, want to focus on doing the work that needs to be done, so you can rely on them to be internal champions around this issue. It is important to recognize that there will be some resistance. Work with people so they have the opportunity to become more comfortable with this type of change. Communicating often and openly and being credible and trustworthy are the two most important leadership behaviors in this situation. Be prepared to meet resistance and have a good strategy to both embrace resistance and then move people through it. In chapter 8 we discuss how to deal with resistance to change in more detail.

Assess Your Library's Capacity for Doing the Work That Needs to Be Done

Fan out across the organization and figure out what people spend their time on during the day or week. As a general rule, people will keep doing the job they have always done, and often in the same way, unless there is a focused effort to stop doing the job the same way. Start asking questions about why people spend their time on certain tasks. Put together a list of key tasks by person and the percentage of time that is spent on each task. This just needs to be a general allocation, not a precise time and motion study. Your goal here is simple: to gain a sense of *what* people are spending time on, *why* they are doing it, and if *continuing to do it* supports the library's goals or no longer serves them. Once you've made this assessment, reallocate people's time and energy to the top goals and away from goals that are lower on the list. Three questions we use with individuals and groups to assess the organization's work habits are:

1. What do we want to keep doing?
2. What do we want to stop doing?
3. What do we want to start doing?

If you are not able to make this change explicit and work through it with people, then either no change will take place or the pace of change will be too slow to be meaningful. Remember to create a sense of urgency for change.

There is an important action that goes with this principle, and that is to help people feel comfortable about not doing or letting go of the "old" work. Often people feel the work they are doing is important, even if it does not fit with current goals and objectives. Perhaps the role was important for a specific purpose, but it no longer serves the primary needs of the library constituents. It's best to be gentle with people and allow enough time for the change. Doing new work or the work that needs to be done can be very difficult for people to accept because it means they must change their own behaviors. Let's look at an example of what it means to be doing the work that needs to get done.

A branch manager is asked to support the library's top goals by spending 20 percent more time meeting with potential library donors and doing fund-raising. The trade-off for the branch manager is to spend less time (a) monitoring the details of the monthly budget reports and (b) acting as a project manager on selected projects. The director, the branch manager's boss, now must reinforce the message that fund-raising is a more important use of the branch manager's time than double-checking the monthly budget reports for accuracy and acting as a pseudo-project manager. The director now needs to focus on fixing the budget accuracy issues so the branch manager can feel good about letting go of that task. The director also needs to encourage the branch manager to delegate her project management responsibilities and use the opportunity to develop the skills of her assistants or department managers. The branch manager also needs assurance that she will not be penalized for not correcting budget mistakes and will be positively rewarded for making the transition to doing more fund-raising.

The other action that needs to take place is making sure the branch manager has the training and skills development to do a good job of fund-raising. The worst scenario is to ask the branch manager to "do the work that needs to be done" and then not invest time and resources into making sure she can be successful. Again, all of this can be outlined in a letter of agreement so that both manager and director have a full understanding of the change and establish clear expectations around the branch manager's new responsibilities.

Principle Three: Relying on the Group as the Primary Unit of Work

Are there a few "go to" people that can pull a project out of the fire? Do you tend to always use the same person in the role of problem solver or firefighter? Do you recognize the contribution of all group members or do you focus on one or two individuals to get the work done? Do you try to develop ways to have all the group's members be accountable or responsible for project goals and team success? In many organizations, including library systems, the culture often rewards the "heroine" or "hero," the person who against all odds always manages to pull off the project, often in the twelfth hour. Of course, everyone is eternally grateful for this person's contribution because without such a heroic effort, the project might never get completed on time. We shower the hero or heroine with praise and acknowledge their "over the top" efforts.

Often this occurs at the expense and psychological harm of other group members, who may have been making their contribution all along during the project but who are not the ones to "rise to the occasion" in such a public manner. In this culture of hero worship, the contributions of other group members go largely unnoticed. In an era when there are fewer resources with which to manage more and more activity, it is critical that leaders figure out how to rely on the group as the unit of work rather than one or two individual heroes who can "pull off the job." In today's environment of change and complexity, all group members can be valuable contributors to projects. The work of the leader is to ensure that all employees make a contribution that both benefits the organization and improves the performance of the group. Remember, heroes need rest and rejuvenation, and they will eventually burn out. It is in the best interest of the employees and the organization to work more effectively as a team or cohesive work unit. Another way to think of this principle is to remember to avoid hero worship on projects and instead focus on harnessing, appreciating, and rewarding the work of all members of a group. You will get better results if you can focus everyone in the group on the project at hand.

The term "team" has taken on a negative connotation lately. Many critics of teams point out that what employees really do is work in groups or ad hoc committees or task forces. When we talk about the "group," we are referring to a collection of people that comes together for a common purpose to work on a project or task that usually has a defined beginning and end. The new reality is that most of our work in organizations involves more than one person, so it becomes critical to success to rely on the group, in addition to key individuals, to get the right work done. Regardless of the language connotations, the point here is to learn how to empower the group to get work done rather than relying on organizational heroes to constantly pull projects out of the fire.

Action Building

The following are the primary actions we want to take to successfully rely on the group as the unit of work.

1. Develop an explicit process for group accountability and responsibility and get commitment and agreement from group members or employees. Individual job accountability and responsibilities already exist in the organization, so start with these and expand them to the group level. Effective group work includes both individual and team accountability. Encourage the group members to develop their own group norms and rules or guidelines at the beginning of each project. Make any agreements and decisions explicit and share them with other people in the organization, especially your customers, partners, and key constituents. When agreements are made "public," group members are likely to be more accountable for their actions and the project's success.

2. Develop a reward system that recognizes both group and individual achievement. If you don't reward it, people will not do it. Figure out ways to have project group members share a common performance objective. As a general rule, you want it to be a stretch objective, where 80 percent of it can be reasonably met and the other 20 percent would challenge the individual or group and take a focused effort to achieve success. Try to develop one or two shared, group-level performance goals for work projects (more than two makes it too complicated for team members to negotiate cross-department or cross-functional turf or political issues).

Tools for Relying on the Group as the Primary Unit of Work

1. Start with the key activities that will get you success. These include:

  a. Library vision statement

  b. Team purpose statement and charter that lists the primary reason the group is together (purpose statement), how the group members are going to work with one another (team charter), and their internal "champion" or project sponsor

  c. Clear success criteria, including metrics and qualitative descriptions of success. Success criteria need to be clear and understandable for all group members, and supported by senior management. Success criteria can also extend over the life of the project. For example, on a web implementation project in a public library, the group developed one success criterion for reaching customer service levels of 95 percent or better six months after the new web system was installed. On the same project, another success criterion was 100 percent of all features implemented within ninety days of the project going "live." Be creative and make sure the success criteria link to the key goals and outcomes. If they do not, then you are not encouraging and rewarding the desired new behaviors and actions of group members.

d. Clarity about group members' roles. Be sure role definitions are written out and agreed to by group members and senior managers. Use an informal letter of agreement or an e-mail memo to write down assumptions and expectations for each group member and for the group as a whole. We will learn more about how to do this when we talk about contribution in chapter 5.

e. A process for making agreements and decisions among team members. Be sure the decision-making process is discussed and understood. Will the group make decisions by consensus, by majority vote, or by group leader with input, or will it use a mixed model depending upon the situation and the level of agreement or conflict among group members? Again, clarity among group members around decision making is important for sustaining healthy group dynamics and moving the project along.

f. Reward and compensation or other incentives are clearly spelled out to group members so they are motivated to reach the project goals and understand the recognition and rewards they receive when they achieve the stated success criteria.

2. As a leader, assist the group with establishing boundary constraints up front. Boundary constraints define the parameters of a project or, in the parlance of the playground, define the sandbox that the group intends to work in for the duration of the project. Be sure boundary constraints are discussed and agreed upon up front with all team members and are revisited at consistent intervals through the life of a project. Typical examples of boundary constraints include the project budget, timelines, dates for key deliverables or tasks, team members' time commitments, access to and use of technologies, access to stakeholders and constituents, and so on. Groups work best when they have a good sense of boundaries—or what they have to work with as they get started on a project. Be sure to update the group if any of the boundary constraints change so the group members can respond responsibly and creatively to any changes.

3. There is a project management maxim that states "go slow to go fast." Remember, it is better to take time up front and establish relationships, build trust, educate group members, and develop a common vision if you want and expect to succeed. It is common for groups to spend one to three meetings on the up-front work of the vision, charter, and purpose statement, decision making, role clarity, and success criteria. Encourage group members to self-organize and offer resources and assistance as needed. Using these tools will put you on the road to success.

Assess Your Library's Capacity for Relying on the Team as the Primary Unit of Work

Start the assessment process by checking to see if the tools described earlier are in place on each of your library projects. If they are not in place, work with the project leaders or the entire group and encourage them to use the tools. Most groups can manage themselves if they know the expectations and are clear about the objectives. Rather than swoop in and demand a reorganization of the group, a better strategy is to work with the group or project leaders and ask them to use the tools. Most groups need input from senior leadership in the areas of boundary constraints and reward and compensation. Be sure to work in partnership and to communicate expectations and information with the group members so they are able to self-manage as much as possible.

Also check to see if there is overreliance on a few individuals. Are there ways and opportunities to reallocate the workload? Can you ask other group members to take on other or different tasks? It might even be necessary for you to talk to your organizational heroes and ask them to stop doing so much. This can be a delicate conversation, since many heroes may derive self-esteem and self-worth from their role. Proceed with compassion and firmness, and help your heroes to find other ways to contribute.

Principle Four: Sharing Information

Do you or the organization have a tendency to limit the number of people who have access to critical information such as budgets, staff reports, strategic plans, or resource planning? Do you routinely share critical information or only distribute it on a need-to-know basis? Do all the members of a project team have access to the budget and the authority to make budget trade-off decisions? Or is the project manager the only person who has the information and authority to make such decisions? Is information shared on a networked basis and available through e-mail or shared file resources, or is it distributed from the top down to select individuals? How do you share information with your constituents, government agencies, local and state governments, and board of directors?

In a networked world, sharing information is critical. Withholding or controlling information results in suboptimal solutions and impedes employees' ability to do their best work because they may not have the information they need to get the job done. A project group, for example, cannot be expected to make the most effective decisions and resource trade-offs unless every member has access to and understands the implications of the project budget. People act more responsibly and make better decisions when they are well informed. Sharing information is directly related to trust. It is important to have trust in people's ability to gather, analyze, and use information to better the library and its services. This is one of those instances where it is better to teach someone to fish than to feed a person a fish you have caught.

Action Building

The following are the primary actions we want to take to successfully share information throughout the library system.

1. Define rules and expectations about sharing information with one another, external partners and vendors, the public, and other audiences.

2. Let go of the need to know everything or tightly control access to key information all of the time. Trust that others will use the information wisely and in ways that support the library's goals and objectives.

3. Consider disseminating information in ways and in forums that support the library's goals and objectives. Invite participation and feedback from diverse sources. If you do, you will end up with a better solution because you have encouraged participation and gained more perspectives to solve complex problems.

Tools for Sharing Information

1. Develop open mechanisms for the routine sharing of information, including

   a. staff meetings

   b. employee meetings

   c. city council meetings

   d. public forums

   e. e-mail server with global e-mail capacity or group e-mail lists

   f. public website and private-side web pages

2. Take time to gather, integrate, and share information across the organization and between organizations.

3. Customize the delivery of key information if necessary and communicate it in the language of the target or intended audience.

4. Have a system that tiers or categorizes information. You can use different criteria—such as informational only, service or fee affecting, donor or fundraising—to communicate information to different audiences. This will also assist you in targeting different audiences with the appropriate information. For example, budgets and the strategic plan are Tier 1. This information needs to be shared throughout the organization and specifically with project members. Announcements of new programs, service availability, and technology enhancements are Tier 2. This information needs to be widely broadcast to the public, key constituents, vendors, and partners. The point here is to use information strategically and openly, and share it in a way that is more focused for each audience. Information sharing ultimately results in more support throughout the library and increased trust from the public and government leaders.

Assess Your Library's Capacity for Sharing Information

Check to see how many of the tools discussed earlier are currently in place and evaluate how you routinely communicate with employees, customers, partners, constituents, and library donors. How can the library benefit from being more open with information, both internally and externally? Are the primary components of the budget and the library's strategic plan shared throughout the organization? Can you remove any restrictions on the use of information? We encourage you to have organization-wide discussions on information sharing. Suggest guidelines or rules around such sharing if necessary. Give people the information they need to make good decisions.

How to Work with the Four Principles

The following are a few good rules to remember as you consider facilitating change in your organization.

1. It is better to start with one or two of the four change principles and apply them on a small scale to start with. Pull a cross-functional group together to develop a SWOT analysis. Include employees, vendors, partners, constituents, and the public in this group. Work with your immediate staff and use the new information to modify strategic initiatives (principle 1). Setting up a pilot project is also an effective way to introduce high impact change. For example, if you are about to initiate a new project, take advantage of the opportunity to bring together resources so you can do the work that needs to be done (principle 2). Consider using a project group that is high-performing and is capable of some degree of self-management to introduce a shared performance goal and success criteria (principle 3). Start sharing information today by making sure employees, especially those working on top project initiatives, have access to budget information that affects the project (principle 4).

2. Change what is not working and keep doing what is working. This way you are not adding to your workload and stressing yourself or the organization.

3. Create success through small wins (Kotter 1996). You want people to feel immediate results and experience success. This builds momentum for change throughout the team and organization. It also helps to mitigate the organization's resistance to change.

4. Last of all, nurture people through the change and provide support at every step. It is our natural tendency to fall back to what we know if things do not always go well or we encounter difficulties along the way. It takes twenty-one days to change a habit. Your role is to listen, nurture, prod, push, and reward change.

4

Connection

*Being connected to people who can open doors, offer
support and backing, provide information, mentor and
teach, and add to one's reputation increases power.
You can increase your own power by forming strategic
relationships, and you can strengthen others in the
same way. Take the time to introduce the staff in your
organization to the people they need to know. Find
ways to connect them to sources of information.*

—Kouzes and Posner 1995

Connection is the new glue of leadership. It is one of the three core leadership actions, along with contribution and collaboration, that fit with our complex organizations and highly dynamic workplaces. When we seek connections with our staff, employees, constituents, partners, and stakeholders we are doing the core work of leadership. As mentioned earlier in chapter 1, *connecting* is a critical leadership skill in today's networked world. Connection is about making the right connections between people and organizations, and using these connections to link people together for a common goal. It is an approach that favors "power with" rather than "power over." Partnerships, cooperatives, project teams, community initiatives, and Internet- or network-based systems are all examples of connection. In connection we are linking or connecting people and resources rather than delegating work to others. Our primary role is to act as the connector, not the delegator. Our job is to look for new opportunities for connection, revisit existing connections to make sure they are the right ones for a current project, and put our staffers and constituents in connection with each other to mine resources and information so they can get the real work done.

Connections can be very dynamic and highly dependent upon the projects, strategic initiatives, or work challenges that are your current focus. Connections start, stop, and are sustained depending upon whether or not they fit with your organization's short- and long-term goals. There are three types of connections: transactional, relational, and social. Transactional connections focus primarily on information or resource exchange for a specific project or purpose. Some of these transactional connections can also be social, but for the most part they exist because there is a need to "get something done." For example, I connect on a weekly basis with Bob, the circulation manager, about the internal web project. We exchange vital information about project details that assists each of us with our project responsibilities. We don't really do much together outside of work, and I don't consider Bob to be one of my confidants, yet we have a good working relationship in the context of the web project.

Relational connections tend to be deeper and represent higher levels of trust and a freer mutual exchange of ideas. Perhaps there is a peer that you trust and partner with in your organization on a regular basis. Or maybe you are partnering with a vendor on a high-risk project—you both have much invested in the outcome—and so are mutually motivated to work closely together to get the job done. Your success depends upon the strength and healthy functioning of the connection or partnership. These relational connections are developed and cultivated both inside and outside an organization. In fact, it is common to develop important relational connections with people outside your immediate sphere of work. It is often easier to develop high-trust relationships with people outside of work because the environment tends to be less political and less prone to breaches of confidentiality and gossip. Leaders also need to develop a few key relational connections internally at their peer level. For example, the director of public services and the human resources manager can benefit from a high-level relational connection because their respective job roles involve many interactions relating to recruiting, motivating, and retaining staff that are crucial to the success of both individuals as well as the organization. Cultivating these relational connections often results in more positive work outcomes because people have high levels of trust and commitment and are more willing to "hang in there" and work out problems or challenges that might otherwise go unresolved if there were only transactional connections.

Social connections represent casual connections or relationships that foster personal and professional growth. Social networks are critical to success because they are also referral networks, and enable leaders to know about and foster connections that might be useful for their staff and constituents. Examples of social connections include your professional networks, people you connect with at professional conferences, donors and library patrons, and golf or social outings with colleagues, board members, and selected internal employees. A library director and a consultant are another example of a positive social network connection. Our social connections introduce us to a wider network of people and resources that can be immediately useful or reap future benefits for us. Some people may be members of all three types of connections, though typically your connections are segmented and serve a specific purpose.

Applications in Action

Starting an Early Literacy Project

An assistant director of a large county public library in Maryland took advantage of the social and political environment to create a successful early literacy project for babies. She connected three related interests and resources from state government, the public schools, and the local management board to build support for a project that benefited mothers and their infants. The assistant director had wanted to start a program for infants and children, but was finding it difficult to get the program going with only library support. She began looking into state and local grants to see if there were similar interests and resources among other agencies and constituencies. She discovered that the state had grants available to support new mothers. The county management board had recently formed an age-based subcommittee that was looking into ways to enhance the state initiative on intergenerational projects for working mothers. With both the state and local resources available, she secured money from the local library foundation to use the mobile library and provide reading services to babies through local child care centers.

She secured a grant to train library staff and conduct research on infant and early childhood development. From the research she and the library team developed a list of bedtime and baby stories that mothers and librarians could read to infants, created early literacy kits to be distributed to child care centers and mothers through the public schools, and received funding to hire a full-time early literacy volunteer program coordinator. The assistant director's ability to recognize the common threads and interests of varying groups and then connect them together in an innovative program to serve a new constituency is an example of connective leadership in action. She comments that she is most proud of bringing people together across the county's branch libraries to create a cross-functional library team. The process was very political and she became an "activist" as she responded to this critical social issue. The work was inspiring, she says, and the connection between the mothers and their babies and the library and child care staff made us "light up all over."

Expanding Connections on Campus

The director of a large state university on the West Coast faced a problem of internal visibility. She describes herself as a middle manager within the larger university system. She realized that her university colleagues—primarily the faculty, adjuncts, and researchers—routinely held meetings and made decisions regarding research and library resources without the presence of any library personnel in the meetings. While she felt her immediate boss was supportive of the library's value on campus, he had not taken any direct action to ensure the library was always represented in key meetings. The director knew the library's resources had expanded substantially in the past year, and she decided to take action by expanding connections among the faculty and staff on campus. She was motivated primarily by her desire to provide excellent service to her constituents—in this case, the faculty, students, staff, and researchers. She knew that certain library services could make campus life easier for them, and realized that they lacked information about new services and programs. She also knew that with budgets being tight, it would be beneficial for the library to have more widespread support throughout the campus if it was to continue expanding services.

In an effort to increase the library's visibility, the director sat down and put together a plan to increase her campus connections. She mapped out all the staff and faculty meetings and assigned herself and her library staff to attend key meetings (an internal transactional connection). She made a few calls and got some agenda time to talk about new library programs and services (an internal transactional connection). She informed her immediate boss, a vice chancellor, and even got time on the executive vice chancellor's agenda to discuss library updates (an internal transactional connection that also set up her social connections). She also reached out to the deans and key faculty by getting to know them and their particular fields of study (an internal relational connection). Over time, the faculty and staff comment to her how the library works so much better for them now. Her incremental approach to building connections outside the immediate library staff enables her to continue receiving key budget dollars for library expansion. Her decision to encourage key staff to attend faculty meetings fosters their connection profiles as well, and serves to strengthen the overall status and visibility of the library system. As she said to me in the interview, "I get to play in all the sandboxes now and see it all come together. My job is to make people's lives better. I take pleasure in fixing problems and like to have the library be a welcoming place on campus."

Connecting through Consortiums to Gain Access to Affordable Online Resources

The library director of a private graduate institute works in a distance learning environment where the faculty and students are dispersed around the United States, Europe, and Asia Pacific and the staff is centralized in California. In another example of partnering and connection, the library director wanted to expand access to digital content yet was faced with limited budget funds. The institute could not afford to purchase digital content as a single entity because the costs to the institute were too high. The director joined a consortium of private academic libraries in California called the Statewide California Electronic Library Consortium (SCELC). SCELC's primary role is to obtain digital resources for its members at affordable rates and work with vendors to implement access to their systems for member libraries. SCELC enables its member libraries (there are approximately seventy members) to gain access to digital content that they otherwise could not afford to purchase on their own. Connection examples like this online consortium are critical to success as libraries work more in partnership to share resources and expand services to their users.

Using the Connection Profile

When I begin a new project, check in on an existing initiative, or run into challenges that require me to resolve complex issues, I use the Connection Profile in figure 4.1 to assist me in mapping out my connections so that I can determine how and who else I might need to bring into my circle in order to be effective and achieve the desired results.

FIGURE 4.1   Connection Profile

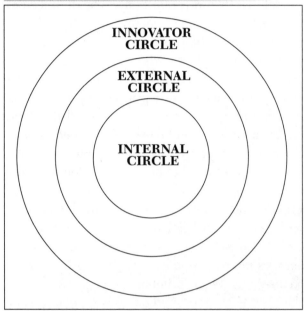

INNOVATOR CIRCLE

EXTERNAL CIRCLE

INTERNAL CIRCLE

Step One:
Mapping My Current Connection Profile

In the "internal circle" of connections, I consider all those I am currently in connection with on a daily, weekly, or monthly basis. Examples include key staff members, my boss, and internal peers, such as other branch librarians or circulation managers. In the "external circle" of connections, I consider people that I am currently in connection with on a daily, weekly, or monthly basis who interact with me or the library staff but who are "outside" the internal system or circle. Examples include primary vendors, local government officials, public school directors, city council members, peer councils, director's club, board members, and so on. In the third circle, or what I call the "innovator circle" of connections, I consider people who represent new opportunities or have the potential for later payoff. Innovator connections might be strategic connections, new connections, or past connections that you want to bring together to work on a new initiative. Use your external connections and do some research to find your innovator connections. Be open to new people or projects that come into your life. An innovator might be a speaker at a conference, the local community college, a city or county agency, a company that wants to pilot new library technologies, or a new board member or recently elected council member.

Step Two:
Adjusting My Connection Profile to Fit the Organizational Need

With a specific project, goal, or task in mind, I go back to my internal circle and do a quick gap analysis. I ask myself the following question: "Who do I need to be in connection with to do the work that is missing from my list?" Maybe I have overlooked a peer that I only see on a casual basis but who now might be integral to my success. Maybe there is an employee who may not be a direct member of my staff but who has key skills and resources that are crucial to success. Or maybe I am in the second phase of a long-term project and I realize that the staff members who were critical to Phase 1 success are not all the same people that will be critical for Phase 2 success. I add these "new" connections to my internal circle. I repeat the process for my external circle and my innovator circle. Again, I ask the question, "Who do I need to be in connection with that is missing from my list?"

There are varying Connection Profiles based on each person's dominant or primary work goals and relationships. Some leaders have fewer key internal connections, numerous external connections, and one or two key innovator connections. Other leaders have numerous internal connections, fewer external connections, and no innovator connections. What is important in profiling your connections is to first know what your goals or desired outcomes are, map your current reality, and then do the gap analysis to determine where you are underrepresented or overrepresented in your connections. The goal is to be in balance relative to your goals, outcomes, or strategic project initiatives.

There are a few general rules to using the Connection Profile and the Connection Profile Matrix (figure 4.2).

1. The broader your leadership role, the more external and innovator connections you need to cultivate. If, for example, you are an executive director whose Connection Profile has many more internal connections than external and innovator connections, then you need to cultivate connections with your external constituents and a few innovators so that you are working at the level of creating and implementing the library's vision. Leading at the vision level means connecting with key constituents, including politicians, the chamber of commerce, the local newspaper, corporations, foundations, and Rotary clubs, in order to make progress on major initiatives, such as building a new library, generating funding for special projects, or adding a "coffeehouse" to your library.

2. If you are a technical professional or individual contributor, your profile will have many internal connections and a few key external connections. You may or may not have innovator connections. Having numerous internal connections means that you are well established in the organization and probably spend a lot of your time working or supporting internal projects. It is healthy for you to

cultivate a few key external connections with vendors, members of your state library association, or academic peers, since these will assist you in your project work and enable you to gain some external visibility in your role.

3. If you are a department head or unit manager, then you will most likely have an equal number of internal and external connections, with at least one innovator connection. As you broaden your scope, your profile changes so that you transition from an internal focus to an external and innovator focus.

4. Your length of time on the job will also determine the number and type of your internal, external, and innovator connections. The longer you have been in the system, the more internal connections are in your profile. Sometimes we lead out of habit and rely on older or internal connections to get our work done. If this shows up in your Connection Profile, then you need to shift toward cultivating external and innovator connections so that you are positioning the library externally for success. Let go of your need to control internal actions and encourage your staff leaders to manage and lead the internal operations.

5. Add a level of sophistication to your Connection Profile by categorizing your connections into the three types—transactional, relational, and social. Doing so provides more detail about the type of connections you need to deepen and cultivate appropriate to your leadership role.

FIGURE 4.2   Connection Profile Matrix—Example

PERSONAL LEADERSHIP CONNECTIONS			
Project / Goal: _____ _____	**INTERNAL**	**EXTERNAL**	**INNOVATOR**
Transactional – Information exchange	– Jane S. – Bill P. – Sally E.	– Peter—web vendor – Bob—city council – Jerry—director	– Sara S.
Relational – High trust – Commitment	– Betty T.	– Chris B. – Steve U. – Wendy O.	
Social – Referrals – Network	– Gwen S. – Cheri R. – Jim M.	– Steve U. – Charles P. – Sally B.	

Figure 4.2 is an example of how to use the Connection Profile Matrix. In this example, I complete the profile with the goals of expanding the library's visibility and figuring out ways to increase the library's value within the county. I want to understand the type of connections needed to be effective. I map out seventeen key connections: seven in my internal circle, nine in my external circle, and one in my innovator circle. Of those seventeen, seven are transactional, four are relational, and six are social. This indicates to me that I have an appropriate mix of connections for my level of leadership for the seventeen connections, but that I have too few innovator connections, given my goals of increasing the library's visibility and value within the county. Secondarily, I probably need to focus my attention on cultivating at least one more internal relational connection so that I build my trust network. As a result, I make the commitment to (a) build a relationship with Victor, a branch librarian whom I have always admired but never taken the time to develop a relationship with; and (b) use my external connections to assist me in finding two people who could be candidates for my innovator circle.

In figure 4.2 I used the Connection Profile Matrix to map out my personal leadership actions. You can use the Connection Profile Matrix Worksheet in figure 4.3 to map out an organizational view of your connective leadership actions. The important point to remember is that effective leaders have a good balance of connections that they can call upon at any time. They build the right con-

---

FIGURE 4.3 Connection Profile Matrix Worksheet

Project / Goal: ———————————— ————————————	INTERNAL	EXTERNAL	INNOVATOR
Transactional – Information exchange			
Relational – High trust – Commitment			
Social – Referrals – Network			

nections or ones that add value to the library system. They do not waste their time on connections that have little payoff to the library. Effective leaders also know when and how to cultivate new connections, revive old connections, and act as a "connection broker" for their staff and constituents. The connection questions listed in the Personal Connection Worksheet (figure 4.4) can assist you in developing your profile and creating an action plan.

Connection Questions for Personal Leadership

As you map your connections on the Connection Profile Matrix, consider each of the questions listed in the Personal Connection Worksheet in figure 4.4 for your personal leadership actions. Respond to the questions with a specific goal in mind. Examples include creating or supporting a bill through the city council, developing an interagency English as a second language program, or developing a leadership training program. Be sure to respond to each question for your internal, external, and innovator connections.

Connection Questions for Organizational Leadership

You can also use the Connection Profile Matrix to map your organizational connections. Consider each of the questions listed in the Organizational Connection Worksheet (figure 4.5) for your organizational leadership actions. Be sure to respond to each question keeping your organization's internal, external, and innovator connections in mind. Again, when we say "connections" we mean partnerships and relationships. As in the personal leadership example, start with a specific goal. For organizational leadership, consider the collective actions your organization needs to take around connection in order to reach its goal. These are typically larger project initiatives, such as a web automation or early literacy project. Internal goals, such as a reorganization within a department or library system or the "reengineering" of an existing customer service process, are also good ways to use the worksheet. Utilize key staff to "fan out" internally and externally to build and leverage connections on a larger scale.

You can thus use the Connection Profile Matrix Worksheet to map out both your personal leadership connections and the library or organization's leadership connections. Doing both helps to clarify how your own leadership actions involving connections can be leveraged to meet the larger organizational goals and objectives.

There are many ways to enhance and sustain your workplace connections. The tools and examples in this chapter are designed to get you thinking about the importance of your current connections so that you can assess how to move forward and develop new connections that further your personal and professional goals. Connection is indeed the glue of leadership because it is the foundation or structure for growth and success. Let's turn now to the second leadership practice, contribution, and examine the ways we can act to cultivate talent and take advantage of the human resources in our libraries.

FIGURE 4.4 Personal Connection Worksheet

1. Who do *I* need to be in connection with to achieve *my* goals? List your primary work connections.

_____

_____

_____

_____

2. Who do *I* need to be in connection with to achieve *my* vision? List the professional people who are essential to your success.

_____

_____

_____

_____

3. Who needs to be in connection with *me?* List the people who might benefit from being connected with you in your professional life.

_____

_____

_____

_____

4. How do *I* form *my* connections?

_____

_____

_____

_____

5. How do *I* sustain *my* connections?

_____

_____

_____

_____

6. How do *I* complete or end *my* connections?

_____

_____

_____

_____

7. As a leader, what other actions can I take to create connections that benefit the library and its goal?

_____

_____

_____

_____

FIGURE 4.5   Organizational Connection Worksheet

1. Who do *we* need to be in partnership with to further our vision? List the connections needed on the broader organizational, library, or department level.

   _____
   _____
   _____
   _____

2. Who do *we* need to be in partnership with to further our goals?

   _____
   _____
   _____
   _____

3. Who are *our* current partners? List your library's important affiliations, partners, and cooperative members.

   _____
   _____
   _____
   _____

4. Why are *we* in connection with these partners? List the purpose or reason for the relationship.

   _____
   _____
   _____
   _____

5. Who would *we* consider to be potential new partners?

   _____
   _____
   _____
   _____

6. Why would *we* want to be in connection with these potential partners? List the purpose or reason for the relationship.

   _____
   _____
   _____
   _____

7. Are *we* perceived as credible by our partners? As leaders, what can *we* do to enhance our library's credibility among current and new partners?

   _____
   _____
   _____
   _____

5

Contribution

We call it fluid leadership. People figure out what they're good at, and that shapes what their roles are. There's not just one leader. Different people lead during different parts of the process. —Al West, as quoted in *Fast Company,* June 2003

The second core leadership practice is contribution. Contribution is also directly linked to the second change principle: doing the work that needs to be done. Contribution is often overlooked as a leadership practice because we tend to assume that everyone is hired to do a particular job. Sometimes we tend to take one another's contributions to the organization for granted. Our attitudes and assumptions about what people are expected to do are so deeply embedded in us that we rarely, if ever, stop to consider how our lack of attention to contribution negatively affects the real work of the organization.

Contribution is about doing good work and the real work that needs to be done. Contribution is fluid and takes advantage of each person's talents at any given time on any given work project or task. The shift we want people to make is to speak about their role in terms of "this is the work I do" rather than "this is my job." When people say they are doing the work it means they are engaged, enthused, challenged, and inspired. Staff, team, or group members are practicing contribution when they are encouraged to set, clarify, and share their expectations about what they can do on a project. By setting and sharing expectations, these people make a commitment and take ownership of their actions. Being explicit about your own contribution means that other group members are knowledgeable about what every other member is bringing to the group. This open information sharing (remember principle 4) helps create trust and interdependency among the group and sets the stage for success.

Leaders who practice contribution focus on and identify the talent or contribution each person can or is willing to make toward a project's goal and outcomes.

Sometimes it might just be making sure the day-to-day work gets done as well: high-quality reference work; responding to the needs of customers while checking books in and out; or making sure that books are shelved in the right place so that customers can find them. But when you are engaged in larger projects, face complex situations, and have challenging goals, leaders need to take a larger view and realize that the entire talents of the library staff are available as resources at any given time to contribute to a given project or to work on a top priority. If you want to leverage all the resources at hand to solve a problem or implement a key project, then you need to lead from this larger viewpoint that places contribution at the front of leadership. This is important because leaders who actively cultivate people's talents and resources enable others to act and get results. It is an aspect of human nature that people will continue to do what they have always done in their jobs unless there is some active intervention to change their behaviors. Not paying attention to contribution means that leaders run the risk of being unable to leverage the available resources to create organizational success.

Applications in Action

Web Migration in a Public Library for the New Automation System

Two managers in a midsized public library system with six branches jointly lead a major migration from a text-based to a new Windows-based web automation system. The city library is also a member of a technology cooperative that serves eight other nearby cities or local jurisdictions. There were two extraordinary circumstances that the project team leaders faced: a compressed time frame and the lack of an automation manager at the cooperative, who would have acted in the role of project director. The coleaders stated that "people knew we were committed. Of course, we had a deadline and not enough people so we had to be involved. This encouraged people to do their part and they understood the project was really going to happen. There was no turning back."

During different parts of the implementation process, the cooperative members had to contend with talent gaps in their efforts to keep to the fast-track schedule. For example, the initial vendor selection team included one to five people from each jurisdiction. Once the vendor was selected and began working with the team, the cooperative members realized that the consultant they had hired to assist in the implementation was not going to be on-site often enough at each of the libraries to be useful in the communication process. To solve this problem, the cooperative "borrowed" a staff member from one of the jurisdictions (another city) and asked her to serve as the lead person to communicate with the vendor, field problems, coordinate tasks, and communicate key information across jurisdictions. This person acted as a project communications manager during the critical implementation stages of the project.

One of the project coleaders had multiple roles. In addition to her own full-time job as a library manager and the time she spent on the new automation system for the cooperative, she was also the project manager on the upgrade program for the personal computers and printers in the city's main library. During different phases of the automation project, she lacked the staff to help her install the equipment and train staff for the project. During critical times she would call upon one of the reference librarians from her library system to assist her. The library manager took the reference librarian off her desk assignments and made her an ad hoc or temporary team member. The manager worked with other library staff to coordinate and reassign their work, which often included traveling back and forth between six locations, in order to coordinate staffing on both projects. The organization became highly fluid in terms of moving staff around based on the critical need at the time. The manager called upon different people at any given time who had the needed talents to contribute to the project's success.

There was also resistance by some staff members who did not want to transition from the current system to the new one. This was amplified by the shorter time allotted for training on the new system. Yet other staff members would train and practice on their own time. The coleaders were always moving people around to free up staff as needed, such as moving someone from the reference desk to take the training or to deliver training. Each person was scheduled an hour a day off the desk to take the training. Everyone said they were too busy: "What are we going to drop out of our schedule?" they asked. The project demands created discomfort because the staff were falling behind and unable to do their jobs full time. This took many employees out of their comfort zone. The daily work was piling up but the web automation project was the library's top priority, even over the day-to-day functioning of the library. The coleaders remarked that "it was difficult for some library staff to recognize there was a need that was greater than what each of them did on a daily basis." They continued to move forward and over time more people began to contribute in meaningful ways to the web automation project.

In terms of leading around contribution, there was a core team of three people who defined what talent and resources were needed for the project at its various stages. It was obvious to the managers that certain people needed to be involved at the beginning, and yet not all of those who needed to be were involved. The managers lobbied to get key people assigned full time for the duration of the project because it was counterproductive not to have them involved at the outset. They talked formally and informally to staff members and to the library director, who felt that people were already overwhelmed. However, they convinced the director that a particular staff person was really needed. It also helped that the staff person wanted to be involved in the project.

Throughout the course of the web automation project, the managers said there were also events that were serendipitous. For example, when it was time to install the Spanish-language catalog, the vendors loaded a software language in the test database that made the database inaccurate and full of errors. One of the managers then sent an e-mail to all staff members as usual when the library system had a new test setup. She told everyone the information was up, asked people to take a look at it, and send comments back to her by the due date. A clerical employee with very good Spanish language skills became very interested and involved in editing the Spanish-language catalog. She spent hours going through all the screens, finding mistakes and making comments and suggestions. When the coleaders heard she had done this, they included her on the committee and she became one of the representatives at the cooperative meetings. The coleaders remarked, "She was at these meetings with very high-level staff and gave suggestions and really assisted us. We were impressed by her poise, her skill and knowledge. It was a surprise to discover talents among people in the library that are really hidden." Examples like these highlight the contributions made by both the project leaders and by different library staff at different points in the automation project's life cycle. This type of complex, larger-scale project is a good illustration of contribution as a universal leadership practice.

Faculty Research Contributions in an Online Academic Library

For this example, let's refer back to chapter 4 and the situation of the library director of a private graduate institute who works in a distance learning environment where the faculty and students are dispersed around the United States, Europe, and Asia Pacific and the staff is centralized in California. He believes that the scholarly output of faculty research is one of the top two critical priorities for the institution. The challenge for the director is to highlight faculty members' research contributions by making the institute's research efforts more available and accessible to the larger academic community. In this case, it was important for the director to create a low-cost strategy that would enable the institute to make a research contribution at a broader level in the academic community.

The problem facing the director is to develop a common repository or database of faculty research and doctoral student dissertations. To achieve this objective, he first uses existing network and information technology to create a data repository to centralize the institute's research work. He also works closely with each of the academic departments and encourages each school and program to begin accepting research and doctoral dissertations in digital form. At the same time, he systematically begins converting research materials from a paper to a digital format. After he establishes the data repository, his external work is to cast as broad a net as possible to the larger academic community so that the institute's research and scholarly output are broadly accessible. In order to do this, the director uses the Internet to make the research available globally at no cost. His efforts to make an organizational contribution are linked to the institute's top goals of funding development and gaining recognition in the larger academic community. This goal is critical because the institute, though well known in its field, needs to broaden its visibility in order to attract grants and other funding and research opportunities.

Leading with Contribution

There are multiple ways to incorporate contribution into your leadership practices. Again, the goal is to take action in ways that make good use of talent in the library so that people's contributions are purposeful and linked to a specific goal, objective, or strategic initiative and the library's top priorities. Saying it another way, it is important that each person understands how his or her daily job responsibilities and work are tied to the library's overall vision, goals, and priorities. Knowing this enables people to better understand how their efforts add value and assists them in making good decisions in their daily work. When this occurs, people take actions that are aligned with priorities. This enables the library to achieve its desired results.

Use the Contribution Checklist (figure 5.1) as a tool to help you assess, reallocate, and recruit talent so that you can maximize your human resources for daily tasks, special projects, and major initiatives and strategies. Listed below are different ways to use the Contribution Checklist for identifying gaps and developing strategies to utilize additional talent and resources.

1. You can use the Contribution Checklist to develop a talent inventory for a specific project, existing program, or major initiative. Complete the checklist by responding to the following questions. (Refer to figure 5.2 for an example of how to use the checklist.)

    a. What talents do we need?

    b. What talents do we have?

    c. What talents are we missing?

    d. What are our strategies to get the talents we need?

2. You can use the Contribution Checklist to make a talent inventory for the whole organization. This is especially helpful when you are doing any type of vision work, developing goals, setting new strategies, evaluating performance criteria, and refining job descriptions.

3. You can use the Contribution Checklist in various stages of a project. For example, use the checklist in the early stages, when you are forming a project group and are trying to identify the right resources and talents required for success. This is especially crucial during the formation or start-up stage of a project. Be sure to address the topic of contribution much as you would address the project's purpose, goals, and success criteria. Make identifying contribution a natural extension of the group formation and project-chartering process.

4. You can also use the Contribution Checklist for existing programs or processes when you need to review or reassess resources or when new customer needs or other requirements demand a change in the program's goals that might require different skills and talents to sustain success. For example, perhaps web customer inquiries have increased to 35 percent of the library's total customer service inquiries. Review the current customer service processes and assess whether or not you have the right talent, training, or staffing requirements to handle the web-based increases. Can the same person manage all the customer

FIGURE 5.1 Contribution Checklist

PROJECT/PROGRAM/INITIATIVE: _____

List of Talents and Resources	What talents do we need?	What talents do we have?	What talents are we missing?	What are our strategies to get the talents we need?
Fund development				
Project management				
Web technologies				
Community advocacy				
Construction and contracting				
Multilingual				
Background in politics				
Specialized knowledge areas				
Other:				
Other:				
Other				

FIGURE 5.2 Contribution Checklist—Example

PROJECT/PROGRAM/INITIATIVE: _____ Web Migration _____

List of Talents and Resources	What talents do we need?	What talents do we have?	What talents are we missing?	What are our strategies to get the talents we need?
Fund development	In budget	Exist—library director	None	Good for now
Project management	Critical need	Two managers who have the talent but are doing other jobs Project liaison	None	Need to reassign two internal managers for project duration—one year Work with cooperative to have single vendor project liaison
Web technologies	Web interface Internet Programming Windows	Web interface and Internet	Automation manager Training	Through cooperative or contract out to fill the gap Extensive internal training before and during implementation with post-training as required
Community advocacy	Critical	Library director and staff	None	Continuous communication posted in public venues to keep community informed
Construction and contracting	Critical	None	Not available at local library	Use cooperative resources
Multilingual	Critical	None that we are aware of at this time	Spanish speaking	Check internally for multi-lingual and add to project team
Background in politics	Helpful if good communication skills	Have this internally with the program managers	None	Good for now
Specialized knowledge areas	Windows technology Spanish speaking	One person in IT known	Windows	Use vendor for Windows training plus internal expertise Check to see if any staff are bilingual and available for project
Other: PC and equipment installation resources	People to install and train staff	Only one person	Need two to three people	Reassign work to other library staff to free up those with training skills Reset priorities and push lower-priority projects out

inquiries? Do you need to train a backup? Or is a different skill set required to handle web requests?

The following are some suggestions for a process to bring contribution into team meetings and the daily work processes. Use this process when you are starting a new project, when it is necessary to review or reassess people's contributions on an existing project, or at a staff meeting when you are working on creating a vision and developing goals and strategies for the library. A couple of good references for leading and working effectively with groups are *Managing Teams* by Lawrence Holpp (1999) and *No More Teams* by Michael Schrage (1995).

1. Bring the group together (remember our motto: get the system into the room). Have a formal agenda for the meeting that lists "personal contribution" with a start and stop time so that people expect this to be an important topic of discussion. It is also helpful to have a facilitator, although the group leader can act as a facilitator if desired.

> a. Be sure to set a context for the discussion by reiterating the vision, goals, or objectives of the program or project. If you are using this process to discuss contribution for a specific unit or department, it is still important for you to outline the rationale for the discussion so that staff members understand why they are discussing contribution. For example, is there a crisis? Are we reallocating job responsibilities? If you do not fully explain the rationale, then people may be suspicious or resistant to having the discussion.

> b. Go around the room and ask each person or group member to say what he or she can contribute to the project and how their contribution makes a difference to the overall project. This is a very effective technique because it helps to clarify assumptions (usually not everyone has the same assumptions) about project roles and leads to the next critical conversation regarding workload (see step c below). It is also very energizing because people have the chance to internalize their own contribution by voicing what they perceive is their value to the project or program. This helps to develop acceptance and agreement.

> c. Clarify and share expectations about each person's ability to commit to their contribution. Here we want to know up front if there are any known limitations or barriers to a person's capacity to contribute to the project. For example, perhaps I can only work full time on the project for three months and after that I am only available for ten hours per week. Or I can be a full-time project member starting next month but not this month. Or I can only make a contribution if the project leader arranges with my boss to have someone cover for my regular work tasks.

2. Next discuss how to identify and implement a shared performance goal that all project members can be accountable for. Be sure the performance goal is interdependent and utilizes each person's contribution. Ideally, the performance goal would not be achievable without each person's unique contribution.

Once you develop a shared performance goal, identify the reward so that the two are linked and members can understand how their contribution is linked to both performance and reward. Using our previous example of the web automation project, a shared performance goal might be 95 percent of database accuracy in the initial cutover. All departments agree to this goal—information technology, reference, catalog, check-in, web and in-person customer service, and so on. Each person is then responsible for defining what 95 percent accuracy means within their function or department and working to reach that shared goal. Once the web automation project members have defined their own contributions around the shared performance goal, then the members can establish a meaningful reward for achieving the objective. Be sure to bring the human resources and other department managers (i.e., staff with budget authority) into this conversation. Establish the criteria for what group members can be rewarded for and what is doable within certain limits. There are always limitations or policies regarding the budget, the union or cooperatives, and human resources policy, so be sure to gather this information up front. Examples of rewards might be bonuses or stipends, time off, trips, and professional development or training opportunities.

One word of caution here is to keep your focus to one (or at most two) shared performance goals, especially if the project is a new concept in your library. People are often challenged to change their behaviors and collaborate in new ways in order to effectively implement even one shared performance goal. Don't overload them with too much. Remember what we talked about in chapter 3. It is better to start with a few steps so that you can generate small wins and build momentum for change.

3. Cultivate talent by implementing a skills development program. Reward people by giving them more opportunities to expand their skills. Have them complete their own Contribution Checklist to assess their areas of development tied to their performance objectives. Use the opportunity to reinforce contribution by sending staff to training courses and conferences. Bring them to high-level meetings to expose them to your contacts. Show them you care about the work they do now and their potential for future contributions. In return the library will be rewarded with enthusiastic and dedicated workers who care about each other and want to contribute as much as they can to the library and its constituents.

If you are interested in learning more about resource staffing and compensation we suggest *Staffing for Results* by D. Mayo and Jeanne Goodrich (2002), *Managing for Results* by Sandra Nelson, E. Altman, and D. Mayo (2000), and *Developing a Compensation Plan for Your Library* by Paula Singer (2002).

Removing Barriers to Contribution

Each of us wants to use our talents and make a contribution, yet we often face real barriers within the library system. Kotter (1996) names four barriers to empowerment that can get in the way of a person's ability to take action. These barriers can slow down and even stop people, including leaders, from making a substantive contribution to the work that needs to get done. As leaders, we want to be aware of these barriers and take action to remove them or mitigate their impact so that people can make the contributions they are committed to for a specific project or in the course of their daily work. The four barriers are (1) a lack of needed skills that undermines action, (2) personnel and information systems that make it difficult to act, (3) bosses that discourage actions, and (4) formal structures that make it difficult to act.

Lack of skills is a critical barrier to project completion and successful contribution. Another way to think about this is to ask, what talents do we need to be successful (on this project or initiative) that we do not currently have on the project? For example, if we are starting a capital campaign for a new library, do we have expertise in fund development? Perhaps we currently have a person on staff responsible for doing fund development, but he has never done fundraising for a capital campaign. Another example is a web migration project. Do we have the necessary network communications expertise or website development expertise in-house, or do we need to acquire the talent some other way? Leaders always need to make an assessment regarding the available talent and determine if it is enough to get the job done. Do the staff already demonstrate competency in a particular area? If not, do we need to go outside for additional talent, such as hiring a consultant or contractor? Do we need to send staff to training or work with a local community college or university to build skills through external programs?

Personnel policies and information systems can be common barriers that inhibit contribution in the workplace. Perhaps a project requires an existing employee to be reallocated or temporarily assigned to another branch or specialty area. Collective bargaining agreements or personnel policies can act as barriers to the organization's need for more flexibility to use specialized resources and its call upon skilled employees to be temporarily reassigned. If this is the case, leaders need to partner with collective bargaining groups and the human resources department to come to some mutual agreement over the flexible utilization of talent. Otherwise the library suffers as a whole because systems and policies are not aligned to deliver results. Information systems are legendary for gathering, tracking, and reporting on metrics that are insufficient for making real-time decisions and taking quick action. Sometimes this lack of information can inhibit the progress of a project group or the day-to-day operations of functional departments like reference, materials handling, and cataloging. One remedy for this is to make sure that someone on the project or in the department has database or report-writing expertise so that the group can continue to make progress.

Managers or bosses who discourage people from taking action are highly problematic. In our interviews and research, people identify outdated management practices as one of the top five leadership issues. Most often these managers are acting in the command and control mode. This stifles action and creativity. It also dampens people's enthusiasm and inhibits employees' desire to

FIGURE 5.3   Personal Contribution Worksheet

1. What is *my* work here? List your primary work contribution.

   _____
   _____
   _____
   _____

2. What are *my* talents? List the unique strengths or skills you bring to the library as a leader.

   _____
   _____
   _____
   _____

3. In what ways do *my* leadership contributions align with the library's vision, purpose, and goals?

   _____
   _____
   _____
   _____

4. Where are *my* leadership contributions not aligned with the library's vision, purpose, and goals?

   _____
   _____
   _____
   _____

5. As a leader, in what ways does *my* behavior inspire contributions from others, such as staff, partners, and stakeholders?

   _____
   _____
   _____
   _____

6. As a leader, in what ways have *I* created compelling reasons for people to make their unique contributions to the library?

   _____
   _____
   _____
   _____

7. As a leader, what other actions can *I* take to create even more compelling reasons for people to make their unique contributions to the library?

   _____
   _____
   _____
   _____

FIGURE 5.4   Organizational Contribution Worksheet

1. What is each of *us* in the group bringing to the table? What are *our* collective talents? List the collective contribution of the group.

    _____
    _____
    _____

2. How is each member of the group contributing to the library's vision, purpose, and goals? For example, if you are thinking about your staff, what is the staff's collective contribution on behalf of the library's vision, purpose, and goals? You can also use a department, program, project, or any collection of people that constitute a group you lead.

    _____
    _____
    _____

3. What talents are absent in *our* library? Our program or project group?

    _____
    _____
    _____

4. What talents do *we* need to access or have within our organization or group?

    _____
    _____
    _____

5. What are *our* strategies for finding new talent? For keeping talent? Cultivating talent internally?

    _____
    _____
    _____

6. What structural barriers, such as job definitions, department or organizational structures (think of your organization charts), outdated management techniques, or lack of skills and training, stand in the way of *us* making *our* contributions?

    _____
    _____
    _____

7. What leadership actions can *we* take to remove or mitigate the impact of barriers on *our* staff? Our program and project groups?

    _____
    _____
    _____

Contribution is indeed a core leadership practice. It requires leaders to be aware and open to opportunities to view the talents of people differently than perhaps we are used to, given our existing structures, policies, systems, skill sets, and management practices. Leading with contribution can change the core of your library because it has a profound and positive effect on staff behavior and motivation. Contribution is a powerful practice for leaders. It has the potential to truly maximize and leverage the talent of the library to meet its mission and vision. Let's turn now to chapter 6, which focuses on collaboration as the third critical dimension of leadership.

6

Collaboration

Collaboration has at last assumed its rightful place among the processes for achieving and sustaining high performance. . . . The winning strategies will be based upon the "we not I" philosophy.

—Kouzes and Posner 1995

Collaboration is the third core competency for leaders. Collaboration is creating a shared understanding and interdependency among people who come together to solve a problem. We use collaboration or apply it as a leadership tool in situations that are complex, new, unfamiliar, and challenging (Schrage 1995). As a general rule, collaboration works best when members come together on a project or initiative that is new and has a certain level of complexity. This newness and complexity create a sense of challenge in solving a new problem. Group members tend to be more open to diverse solutions when they realize that the problem at hand is more complex or is unfamiliar to them and can't be easily solved using current or past designs. As a result, group members tend to take more time to analyze and assess the perceived problem when they are confronted with new situations. Collaboration is also a way to do the same work differently. For example, you can use the collaborative process to acquire a bookmobile and provide resources in the community with existing staff. Many libraries are becoming increasingly team-based and use collaboration as part of their problem analysis and design process when studying an issue, e.g., collections or creating marketing strategies.

During the collaborative process, group members form interdependent relationships with other members because they must rely on other team members' talents and contributions in order to meet the overall project goals and objectives. Complexity and newness can, and often do, create anxiety for some group members and cause the group to fumble and stumble at the project's outset. This is considered part of the normal process for group formation. However, leaders do need to pay attention to this dynamic and intervene if necessary to get the group back on course if the group starts faltering too much. Holpp's *Managing Teams* (1999) offers helpful strategies and techniques for fostering good team dynamics and coping with conflict and change.

Collaboration, partnering, and community building are listed as one of the top ten trends for library networks (Laughlin 2000). Cooperatives are a good example of collaboration and partnering in action. Let's consider three examples of collaboration, two in a public library and one in an academic library.

Applications in Action

Web Migration in a Public Library for the New Automation System

Let's refer back to the two managers in a midsized public library working on the web migration project as described in chapter 5. There are several examples of collaboration that proved essential to their success. For example, the vendor for the automation system was selected by all the members. They worked together to define the criteria and both individually and as a group discussed the extent to which each vendor met their needs on each criterion. Group members were able to "see" the different pros and cons of the vendor proposals. As a result, they had more information with which to make an intelligent and effective decision that each member endorsed on behalf of their library. Each library then implemented the automation system internally, within its library or jurisdiction, and worked collaboratively with other cooperative members throughout the design and implementation process.

Due to pressures created by the compressed timeline, the cooperative members did not have time for as many face-to-face meetings as they had in past projects. Therefore, the cooperative team had to develop other means of decision making and consensus development. When they first met, they discussed communications and consensus-generating techniques to support this fast-track implementation process. They did much of their work through electronic discussion lists; each committee had a discussion list and committee members would work online and collaboratively. One person put something up on the list, other members provided input, and another person analyzed the responses and proposed a recommendation. Communications were accomplished almost exclusively through e-mail. All of these group norms and issues about how members would communicate throughout the project were openly discussed and agreed to in advance during the group formation stage in their initial meetings.

The managers remarked that the cooperative members came to consensus surprisingly well:

> Our group came prepared to the meetings and we were influential in who we chose and in the way we designed the options, such as the web catalog. We were prepared. We would talk about the agenda ahead of time, decide the key

things we wanted, and what were our priorities. We came to the meetings and gave cogent arguments why we would do this. Other libraries did not have the staff and did not always have time to figure it out ahead of time.

There were also different levels of expertise in terms of management experience and technical expertise among the cooperative members. Some jurisdictions sent more representatives as a way to expose their staff and get them involved and on board with the project. As the managers explained it:

> We had to collaborate! For example, there were different levels of customer service expectations among the jurisdiction members. For some members the service levels were fine but for us they were unacceptable. Others cared about this issue yet had a different level of what they expected to provide to the customer. For example, we lease books and we do the order processing outside the acquisitions model where you order things. So when we placed the order it wouldn't show in the catalog that we had ordered it. These are the best sellers. Our customers are used to seeing that there are twenty-five copies on order and then placing their hold so they are in line for it before it arrives. For the other libraries it wasn't a priority that the public couldn't see the number and status of copies. They just told people it is on order. But we have people remotely who want to place holds and need to have this visible. So we worked out a solution for us and it turned out it was a good solution for them as well. There could have been the tendency to provide a least common denominator solution, but the public interface issues were critical to us. We obtained 90 percent of what we needed to serve our public.

Throughout the project people were engaged at different points on investigative work to test the database and correct errors. Something would not work in reference and they would talk to someone in interlibrary loan. Those staff members would work on it collaboratively, across processes, to test holds, requests, and so on. Staff on their own would devise tests and report step-by-step on what happened during the test. The managers remarked: "You would see two or three people huddled together at the screen trying to figure things out. They would investigate and give their opinions. This happened at all levels, people providing documentation and working together to solve the data problems."

As one might expect, there was a difference in organizational structures among jurisdictions. For example, each library had a problem log or complaints, but some did not have the problem-solving capacity that the city library had. "People felt they could make a change if they could figure out the problem. They saw that we were making changes in the database and realized they could contribute," the managers commented. "Literally six months into it everyone knew the database better; they knew its limitations and benefits, and understood how each of the changes worked. It was a collaborative process with staff in order to get solutions." These were people who got together, even though they did not ordinarily work together, and made connections that do not always happen in the day-to-day operations. These connections allowed them to act collaboratively to gain new knowledge and achieve results. The managers said they still continue to work together, both formally and informally now, because the nature of the new automation system makes it necessary for departments to work together to solve new problems as they make system upgrades and enhancements.

Sharing of information was critical. Information was shared among all the public library staff on a regular basis. The team created communications processes where there were none so that both team members and users were informed and updated along the way. They used e-mail for updates and were visible throughout the project, going to departments and branches and speaking with staff, attending staff meetings, and doing brown bag lunches. In the early stages, the project managers felt there was almost too much information for people to digest and take in, so they often repeated critical information at different intervals to make sure staff and users knew when key system testing occurred. Three months after the system was installed, the managers sent trainers out to every department and branch library to ensure that staff knew how to use the new system. This comprehensive approach to communications eased the anxiety of the staff, kept people on track for deadlines, and helped to overcome resistance to the new system.

Internal Collaboration

In an example of internal collaboration in this same project, the local project managers needed to design a new home page for their jurisdiction. Internal project members included a computer technician, a reference librarian, a librarian with automation experience, and one of the two project managers. Two members of the team worked with the public and two did not. The two who did not were concerned with systems security, while the two who did were concerned with how the public would use the page features and with ease of site navigation and the user interface. "So we had to collaborate and make one another understand why it was important to have certain elements in the design. For instance, the computer people did not want a bunch of pop-up windows to come up, but we know that if you are at a site and going step-by-step, you have to be able to go from window to window, click on a link, and copy and paste. It was an issue of security versus letting the public do as much as they can," remarked the manager. This subteam worked together to determine the limits of the home page design. They learned from one another's perspective and eventually reached a design outcome that was acceptable in terms of both security concerns and public ease of use.

Collaboration in an Online Academic Library

A library director who works for a private academic institution is responsible for the library resources for faculty, staff, students, and alumni. All of the library's resources are online. When the director first started three years ago there was one centralized online database. Over time the library graduate institute added subscriptions to over ten external databases. For the library director, the challenge was to integrate these disparate databases so that the users—staff, faculty, students, and alumni—could use a single user ID to access the growing number of online resources. The library director was responsible for an effort to deploy a proxy server that would only require a single password and ID. In order to move the project along, the director collaborated with the institute's information technology (IT) department. One of the primary goals of the implementation was to simplify access so that IT staffing could sustain an acceptable level of user support while providing the desired level of customer service for students. For example, the IT staff could not possibly handle support calls for users who were trying to enter into ten different online databases. They simply did not have enough people to handle the calls. The constraint around help desk support staffing and limited budgets pushed the two departments—library services and IT—to collaborate to find an institutional solution that met the needs of both departments as well as provided more expeditious service to students.

The Primary Components of Collaboration

The primary components of fostering collaboration are developing cooperative goals, seeking integrative solutions, and building trusting relationships (Kouzes and Posner 2000). Developing cooperative goals means supporting reciprocity, or helping others as they help you, so that you create and are engaged in mutual reciprocity. This is essential to building trust in your collaborative relationships. It also means that for some projects and initiatives, we emphasize long-term payoffs over short-term gains if the long-term payoffs align with our vision and we see these as the right direction. For example, perhaps the collections department wants funds for automation and there is also a plan to start a multicultural program. These are two important initiatives but there are not enough funds to start both in the same year. So the group makes a trade-off, starting one initiative in the first year and the second initiative in the next year. This trade-off agreement is discussed and agreed to by team members, and then followed through in both years. Part of developing cooperative goals implies owning the goals and making a commitment to seeing them through to successful completion. The process involves looking at the bigger picture while both taking action on the stated goals in the library's strategic plan and meeting the operational needs of the community and customers. As we discussed in chapter 4 on connection, building and sustaining connections are critical to leadership effectiveness and success. Here we are building upon our connections to go one step further and identify those connections or relationships that are collaborative and require mutual reciprocity so that all parties are successful at accomplishing their goals.

Seeking integrative solutions implies that all parties put their ideas, needs, and proposed solutions "on the table" and everyone seeks to form an integrative solution that incorporates each party's or organization's primary needs. Scarce resources always make it difficult for each party to obtain all of its needs and wants. If this is the case, it is critical to have a clear sense of priorities so that the most important needs are expressed and acted upon. "With integrative solutions, people change their thinking from an either/or (or zero-sum) mentality to a positive perspective on working together" (Kouzes and Posner 2000, 160). Technology cooperatives that serve the needs of multiple libraries (and often local governments) are a place where integrative solutions play a key role in determining success as defined by all the cooperative's members. The web automation project and early literacy project we described earlier are good illustrations of the different ways integrative solutions can be designed and implemented. Underlying the capacity for developing integrative solutions is the need to focus on gains rather than losses and the need for open sharing of information and resources among members. Here again, we see that the fourth leadership principle—sharing information—is a fundamental aspect of effective collaborative leadership.

Building trusting relationships means that we work to earn and gain the trust of our staff and constituents. At the core of collaboration is the third principle—relying on the group as the unit of work. For collaborative work, leaders need to be, and be perceived as, honest and trustworthy by all group members if they are to be considered credible leaders and partners. Building trust means that we are open to others' ideas; we display our own vulnerability by taking risks; we listen attentively and openly, without judgment or blame; and we commit to the challenge (Kouzes and Posner 2000). Groups that create, cultivate, and act in trust are also high-performing groups (Holpp 1999). Trust is an essential element of high performance and excellence. Therefore, your chances of success are much greater if you can provide leadership and support in ways that build and promote trust.

Collaboration becomes a core leadership action and a way of being that fosters connections and encourages group members to make substantive contributions to the project. Taking on a collaborative mind-set is critical for leaders. We have to think, act, and breathe collaboration if we expect to take full advantage of our library's talents and resources. Getting to the "we not I" philosophy takes time and practice. The following questions are intended to assist you in assessing your preference for collaboration.

Collaboration Questions for Personal Leadership

Consider each of the questions in the Personal Collaboration Worksheet (figure 6.1) for your personal leadership actions involving collaboration. Use your responses to develop ways to do more collaboration in the service of your vision and goals.

Collaboration Questions for Organizational Leadership

Consider each of the questions in the Organizational Collaboration Worksheet (figure 6.2) for your organizational leadership actions that involve collaboration.

FIGURE 6.1 Personal Collaboration Worksheet

1. Who do *I* need to collaborate with to achieve my vision? List the primary people or organizations you need to personally collaborate (or be in mutual collaboration) with to realize your vision.

   _____

   _____

   _____

2. Who do *I* need to collaborate with to achieve my goals? List the primary people or organizations you need to personally collaborate (or be in mutual collaboration) with to achieve your goals.

   _____

   _____

   _____

3. Who needs to be in collaboration with *me* to achieve the library's vision and goals? List the people or organizations that you believe will benefit from a collaborative relationship with you and the library.

   _____

   _____

   _____

4. As a leader, how do *I* promote collaboration with my staff or peer group?

   _____

   _____

   _____

5. As a leader, how do *I* promote collaboration across departments? With external agencies?

   _____

   _____

   _____

6. As a leader, in what ways have *I* created compelling reasons for people and groups (internally and externally) to act collaboratively?

   _____

   _____

   _____

7. As a leader, what other actions can *I* take to create even more compelling reasons for people and groups to act collaboratively?

   _____

   _____

   _____

FIGURE 6.2   Organizational Collaboration Worksheet

1. Who are *we* in collaboration with currently? List the projects, programs, and initiatives and identify your collaboration partners, e.g., city council, county agency, appointed or elected officials, funders, trustees, state library association, cooperative, and so on.

   _____

   _____

   _____

2. Who else do *we* (the library) need to be in collaboration with to achieve *our* vision? List the primary people or organizations the library needs to collaborate (or be in mutual collaboration) with to realize the vision.

   _____

   _____

   _____

3. What is the purpose of *our* collaboration? List the benefits of a collaborative partnership for both parties.

   _____

   _____

   _____

4. In what ways are *we* demonstrating credibility with our partners?

   _____

   _____

   _____

5. How is *our* collaboration making a difference for *us*?

   _____

   _____

   _____

6. What processes, structures, and programs can *we* put in place to effectively promote collaboration internally?

   _____

   _____

   _____

7. What leadership actions can *we* take to promote collaboration externally among *our* current and potential partners?

   _____

   _____

   _____

Be sure to respond to each question for the organization's top goals, initiatives, or projects. Again, when we say "collaboration" we mean bringing people together to create a shared understanding so that they work interdependently to solve a problem. For organizational leadership, consider the collective actions the organization needs to take in order to function in a collaborative manner.

In the last three chapters we focused in depth on each of the three leadership practices—connection, contribution, and collaboration—and provided useful tools and suggestions for how to implement these practices in the workplace. Gaining the personal and organizational capacity to skillfully lead using each of these core practices as your foundation can improve your personal and organizational effectiveness. In chapter 7 we "put it all together" by looking at ways to integrate each of the three core leadership actions in your library.

7

Putting It All Together

Integrating Connection, Contribution, and Collaboration

If you truly want to understand something, try to change it. —Kurt Lewin

In the previous chapters we have focused on each of the primary leadership actions—connection, contribution, and collaboration—and treated each action individually in order to gain a deeper understanding of what each action entails and how to apply it in your library system. In this chapter we turn to the integration of these primary leadership actions and describe how they can work in combination as an integrated leadership framework. We will start with a case study of a library system where all three leadership actions were applied successfully; introduce two integrative tools that can help you bring these leadership actions together in your day-to-day work; and provide key tips on how to successfully integrate connection, contribution, and collaboration.

Application in Action

A large urban library system composed of a central library and seventeen branches used integrated leadership to achieve its goal of community outreach in one neighborhood. The result was the revitalization of a neighborhood branch library and the increased viability and credibility of the library with community and city leaders. The central library director, who was the branch manager at the time of the project, described the internal and external challenges facing the project. The higher-level leadership challenge was to change the branch library from an internally to an externally focused organization. The goal was to have library staff listen more to the needs of community leaders and customers, and use this input to figure out creative ways to bring the public into the library. This was a different way of behaving for the staff, many of whom tended to work at providing traditional library services, such as circulation and reference, for a "distressed and neglected community." Users had little incentive to go into the library and use services that were not tailored to meet the needs of the local community. Because the library was not offering services that meant something to the users, the branch manager observed that the library had less of an impact than other community organizations serving the neighborhood. The branch manager knew her other external challenge was to enhance the library's position in the community by demonstrating its value to community users.

Early on in the project, the branch manager took a leadership approach based on connection and collaboration to respond to these challenges. She immediately mapped out the primary relationships she would need to build to improve the situation: connecting with key community agencies such as the police, mental health department, churches, community leaders, and educational institutions. The desire to connect with community agencies and leaders was also driven by the opportunity to apply for federal funding and use those dollars for community and library programs that were designed to better serve the constituents. At the time, there was a federally funded program that focused on community revitalization. Communities could apply for funds if they were designated as "weed and seed" neighborhoods. Gaining the "weed and seed" designation enabled local agencies to receive seed money for revitalization. Working together in connection and collaboration with her new community partners, the branch manager assisted in developing a comprehensive study of community problems and issues that ultimately resulted in the community receiving significant funds for rebuilding. The library worked side by side with the police department, social services, community agencies, and the local community college. This initial phase of the project took nearly two years to complete and the team was successful in gaining the "weed and seed" designation for the neighborhood. Working as collaborative community partners, the group mapped out the critical service needs and then developed a multiyear action plan for the next phase of the project. Through this process, the director had built credibility and trust that ultimately led to success when the community group turned its energies to program development and delivery.

Once the initial stage was completed, the branch manager and her staff continued their outreach activities in the community. They worked with the local business and neighborhood associations to coordinate community fairs that focused on bike safety, health, and library services for early literacy. The neighborhood had many immigrants, so bilingual services and ESL (English as a second language) programs were important in improving the health and welfare of the neighborhood. The library staff, who had always worked in isolation from the community, began to work interdependently and collaboratively with other community agencies. For example, they started a partnership with the local community college; the library provided the physical space and the community college instructors taught the ESL classes. As part of the ESL program delivery, the collections department created a learning center in the library to better serve its ESL constituency. As the programs grew, it became apparent to the branch manager that library staff who were bilingual needed to be in more contact with the users. Bilingual library staff were behind the counter working in areas such as circulation and reference. Job descriptions and responsibilities were modified so that bilingual staff could conduct multilingual storytelling, crafts, and other interactive activities. A program called Dia de los Ninos (Children's Day) was designed to take the library out into the community. The program featured children's art, puppet shows, school art projects, and a reading program. "I Like to Read" buttons were distributed in ten different languages. These new programs mobilized different segments of the community. The library continues its work in community outreach and has learned a critical competency—how to better meet the needs of a diverse population. After five years, library staff can hardly keep up with the demand and new ideas. The neighborhood users, community organizations, and the branch library continue to thrive.

The Experience of Successful Integration

The library branch manager reflected on the many learning experiences and surprises that seemed to characterize the library's success in this neighborhood. While she did not use the terms "connection, contribution, and collaboration" in our interview, her story illustrated the effectiveness of these three leadership actions in the library system. All of the key lessons learned by the manager and her staff are linked to connection, contribution, and collaboration. Early on, she asked herself two key questions. First, what is my role as the "face" or leader of the library within this community? Second, what is my own contribution or role as a leader? Operating with the goal of increasing the library's effectiveness and visibility, the branch manager saw her primary role as building closer ties to the community. Building closer ties meant being closer to her branch patrons and better understanding their needs. As a result of her focus on connection, she and the staff were able to deliver programs and services in ways that mattered most to their clients or customers.

The branch manager described herself as "bringing openness" to the process, especially in the early days when community leaders were working to secure "weed and seed" funding. She also experienced tension in her role. For example, on the one hand, the community saw the library as a safe place, a kind of oasis in the neighborhood, where people could come into the library space and feel safe from crime. On the other hand, the branch manager saw the library as not necessarily a safe place, since the library had no way of signing people in and out and providing high levels of security. She began to identify these types of tensions in her role as leader, and developed a rule that guided her leadership actions. She learned to ask herself how much and in what areas the library should give to the community and not give to the community in order to maintain its mission.

The branch manager and staff learned several other important lessons. First, that it can be extremely powerful to put together a set of stakeholders because together the group created many more interesting and unique ideas for programs and methods of delivery than the library could have done on its own. Second, the branch manager, who admitted her bias toward quick action, learned to slow down as a result of working more collaboratively. She discovered that being engaged in the collaborative process meant that the larger group moves more slowly than an individual or a smaller group of people. This deliberate pace, however, provided for greater input and dialogue, and ultimately resulted in outcomes that were greater than what the library could achieve with its own resources. The branch manager remarked that the outcomes were different than she had initially imagined, and yet better than what she had thought would occur. Third, the library's contribution and standing as a community partner was only possible because she and her staff chose to "go deeper into our community and invest in the relationships."

During the early phase of the project, the branch manager was also faced with the challenge of motivating library staff to step forward and create different ways to contribute their skills and knowledge. She began by identifying the available talent within the library staff and assessing how it was currently being used. As mentioned earlier, she discovered staff who were bilingual, yet their jobs kept them from more interaction with the public. She quickly developed a process for job sharing, cross-training, and reallocation that allowed key staff to take a larger role in working with the public. Due to the library's history of not working very closely or in partnership with other community agencies, many staff had not had the opportunity to be involved in public programs. They contributed by expanding their department services, such as collections, and utilizing other skills, such as storytelling or developing an early literacy program. The staff gradually became more aware of how they were contributing to the whole—in this case, the larger goal of neighborhood revitalization. They began to ask themselves what they could do to be their best. They were dedicated to the mission and delighted to be able to make a more visible contribution in the community.

The branch manager, who is now working in a new role as interim library director, continues to implement and practice integrative leadership. She uses a formal process for coaching her leadership team by setting priorities, linking staff actions to key initiatives, and setting goals or metrics for levels of service. She strengthened the implementation of the library's strategic plan by linking it with each staff member's individual performance plan. Part of the performance plan now identifies the ways in which each staff member contributes to goals that benefit the library system. She refocused her team on outcomes and made improvements to the budget process so that resources are allocated to top projects. Although there are always more projects than funds, together her team decides which projects get funded in which year. This greatly increases collaboration across different departments. For example, managers know that the materials handling project gets funded in one year and the reference services project will receive funding the following year. The director also instituted a workload committee to review all library operations and processes and recommend core areas that need reengineering and efficiency improvement. These are all examples of ways to effectively implement and integrate connection, contribution, and collaboration to achieve results in your library. Let's look at key tools and techniques that can assist you in developing your own action plan.

Integrating Personal and Organizational Leadership

We recommend three methods for integrating personal and organizational leadership actions around connection, contribution, and collaboration.

1. Use the Evolving Leadership Practices Assessment introduced in chapter 1. Go back to your results and review your score on each of the three leadership dimensions. For example, let's say you scored high on collaboration and lower on contribution. One action you can take is to identify contribution as a developmental goal for your own leadership. Use the Personal Connection and Organizational Connection worksheets in chapter 4 to identify your top two or three actions to strengthen contribution. Repeat this process for each of the three leadership actions.

2. Another related action is to find out who among your staff or within the library system is proficient at contribution. You can do this by having your staff share the results of the Evolving Leadership Practices Assessment and see who has a strong preference or gift for contribution. Partner with him or her on organizational initiatives as a way of bringing in a leadership attribute, in this case contribution, that is needed within the organization but may not be your strength (at least until you get better at doing more contribution). This action is very effective because it leverages the resources and capabilities of the whole group. It also demonstrates to others your willingness to share leadership and recognize key leadership traits within the library staff.

As we mentioned in chapter 1, initial results from the assessment show that we are typically more developed in one or two of the core leadership practices but not all three. It can be difficult to fully integrate all three core leadership practices within a single individual, so be sure to utilize the skills of everyone in the group to accomplish your goals. As long as the group or team contains within it these three core leadership actions, then you can achieve integration throughout the organization at the same time that you are developing your own leadership competencies. Each of us individually does not have to be proficient at everything as long as these competencies are encouraged and leveraged throughout the organization. As a good friend of mine says, this is why we work in teams.

The Personal Approach to Integrated Leadership

In addition to the first two methods, you can use the following integrative tools or frameworks to assess how you and the organization can act within a framework of integrated leadership. The first tool, the Personal Integrated Leadership Worksheet (figure 7.1), is a good framework to use when you want to do a quick assessment of your current actions and challenges.

FIGURE 7.1   Personal Integrated Leadership Worksheet

My Behaviors and Actions	What am I currently doing?	Where am I currently challenged?	What are my development goals?
Connection			
Contribution			
Collaboration			

Use the worksheet to identify what you are currently doing as a leader in the areas of connection, contribution, and collaboration. For example, let's say for connection you list that you hold regular staff meetings, meet consistently with two city administrators, Jim and Lisa, and outreach to your peers at conferences. For contribution, you list your talent in setting vision and aligning strategy with goals, and for collaboration, you list your work as a member of a citywide sub-committee and your partnerships with the local university. Next identify where you are challenged in each of the three leadership dimensions. For example, under connection you list your lack of outreach with other important city and community leaders (you realize you need to expand beyond your circle of two). Under contribution, you list your desire to take your strategy and vision-setting skills to the next level by engaging in setting a vision for a citywide coalition. Under collaboration, you list your tendency to not delegate more responsibility to your staff and your tendency to control the staff agenda. Once you have identified your current and desired state, you have now created a gap analysis that can lead you to identify potential areas of personal leadership development.

Complete the Personal Integrated Leadership Worksheet by listing no more than two or three actions for personal development under each area. Be sure to keep in mind that our actions are often guided by our role as much as our own personal interests and preferences, so feel free to focus on what has meaning and interest for you at this time in your career and stage of life. See an example of a completed worksheet in figure 7.2.

Depending upon our work environment, sometimes our leadership roles are a natural fit with collaboration. For example, if you are a member of a cooperative you would likely be doing more collaborative leadership. Perhaps you are a member of a peer-level committee who is developing recommendations for how to share new technologies. The success of the committee work largely depends upon the capacity of committee members to work together (collaborate) to achieve success. Our suggestion here is to identify and start with the one or two core practices that you have some proficiency in, then gradually add to your skills by developing the other core practices over time. Set up your own development path and timeline. Use an ongoing or new work initiative to develop other core leadership practices. Seek out opportunities that you feel have the potential to challenge you to grow and learn new skills.

FIGURE 7.2 Personal Integrated Leadership Worksheet—Example

My Behaviors and Actions	What am I currently doing?	Where am I currently challenged?	What are my development goals?
Connection	Hold regular staff meetings Meet with Jim and Lisa (city administrators) Peer outreach at ALA/PLA	Only have primary relational connections with 2 city council members and key community stakeholders	Develop 2 innovator connections in next 90 days Hold open house and invite council and community leaders
Contribution	Vision setting Aligning strategy and goals with vision	Want to expand vision setting skills to city-wide level to assess future needs	Offer my vision setting skills as part of the data gathering and community dialogue around City 2025
Collaboration	City committee on planning and development Digital media project with community college	Sometimes too micro with staff, e.g., agenda setting Tend to take on too much when I could delegate	Ask staff members to set staff agenda—rotate responsibility Reassess workload and figure out ways to offload projects to staff who want more development opportunities

The Organizational Approach
to Integrated Leadership

As leaders, we also want to consider how to take integrative action at the organizational level. Our libraries, like all organizations, exhibit culturally based attributes that influence our personal behavior and actions. The Organizational Integrated Leadership Worksheet (figure 7.3) is a framework for assessing your leadership actions from the perspective of the library as a whole system or broader organization.

As a leader, it is always important to look at leadership from this larger organizational perspective so that you are able to make changes that affect the whole library system, not just the individual. The degree of risk taking or innovation in your library, the way you make decisions, whether or not you value contribution—these are all examples of organizational characteristics or patterns that ultimately reinforce desired (or in many cases, undesirable) behaviors and actions. As we described in our integrated leadership application in action, one of the manager's goals was to transition the library from being an internally to an externally focused organization. She recognized that this type of change needed to happen at the organizational level. This is a good illustration of organizational integrated leadership. You can also refer back to the four principles of change and decide which one is an important lever for affecting organizational change.

Although you can fill out the Organizational Integrated Leadership Worksheet as an individual, we suggest you use the collective approach and complete the worksheet with a department, staff, or cross-functional group. Repeat the process described above as you fill out the worksheet. For example, you identify the reference desk's service level efficiency initiative as your starting point. The current situation can be described as follows. More and more reference inquiries have been coming to the library over the Internet. Currently, the reference librarians are assigned to respond to in-person requests first. Yet the growth in web inquiries has increased so much that they are now nearly 50 percent of all reference desk inquiries. It is apparent that the role and scope of the traditional reference desk has to change in order to respond to all users and within identified service levels.

To focus upon improving your skills in connection, under connection you list that you have started to hold regular project meetings, and you have met with colleagues in other libraries to identify their best practices in this area. For contribution, you list the group's collective talents in data gathering and problem solving, and for collaboration you list the library's involvement in working closely with high-frequency library users to gather input. Next identify where you are challenged in each of the three leadership dimensions. For example, under connection you list the library's overall lack of connection with leading-edge vendors in web and reference technologies. Under contribution, you list the knowledge gap in implementing a virtual reference desk system and the lack of training for reference librarians in the system. Under collaboration, you list the library's lack of active participation in committees or task forces that have been looking at best

FIGURE 7.3   **Organizational Integrated Leadership Worksheet**

Our Project/Goal/Major Initiative:	What are we currently doing?	Where are we currently challenged?	What are our development goals?
Connection			
Contribution			
Collaboration			

practices in referencing and the tendency of the group to be internally focused. As you did in the Personal Integrated Leadership Worksheet, create a gap analysis that leads to potential areas of organizational leadership development. Complete the worksheet by listing no more than two or three potential areas for organizational development under each mode of practice—connection, contribution, and collaboration—that will move the project or initiative forward. See figure 7.4 for a complete worksheet example.

Additional Tools That Improve Integration

Another approach to integration involves not only actions but key processes and supporting technologies. The Integrated Applications Matrix (figure 7.5) lists ideas and examples of actions, processes, and supporting technologies that support connection, contribution, and collaboration. Like the other worksheets, you can use the Integrated Applications Matrix for any project, goal, or major initiative.

In this worksheet we have added the categories of processes and supporting technologies that are critical to the successful implementation of personal and organizational change. We have suggested different ways to apply and implement both processes and supporting technologies so that you achieve your desired results. This matrix can be used for projects or strategic initiatives as diverse as a capital campaign, a bond issue, a multilingual collections project, or an automation project. Key actions, processes, and supporting technologies are listed for each of the three leadership practices.

For example, in figure 7.5 we list specific actions you can take to promote connection:

- developing strategic alliances
- creating external partnerships with key stakeholders
- joining or starting a cooperative
- doing more outreach to the Hispanic or Russian community as illustrated in our neighborhood example at the beginning of the chapter

Under processes that support connection, examples include:

- community meetings or town halls where community members have the opportunity for input
- web pages and links that enable access and greater information sharing
- going to or holding professional conferences and community fairs
- scheduling weekly or monthly staff meetings

Supporting technologies for connection include:

- intranet forums and discussion folders (internal e-mail or discussion areas)
- web-based conferences (commonly called webinars)

FIGURE 7.4 Organizational Integrated Leadership Worksheet—Example

Project Initiative: Reference Desk Service Level	What are we currently doing?	Where are we currently challenged?	What are our development goals?
Connection	Initiating project meetings Starting to meet with colleagues to discuss best practices in this area Doing web search	Don't have good contacts or relationships with leading vendors in web and reference technologies	Develop list of leading vendors and request information meetings to get ourselves educated Leverage our peer contacts outside the system
Contribution	Data gathering Problem solving	Little knowledge in implementing a virtual reference desk system Low skills for reference librarians and staff in virtual technologies	Build skills competency in virtual reference desk service and systems Hire expert consultant to bridge the competency gap
Collaboration	Working with high frequency users to gather input and discover unique needs	Lack of substantive involvement by staff in consortiums or cooperatives in this area Tendency to be internally focused and not actively involved in external groups	Become active on PLA/ALA subcommittee work on web technologies Join a technology affinity group for industry to gain crossover knowledge

FIGURE 7.5 Integrated Applications Matrix

Application Examples: Capital campaign, Multilingual collections catalog, Web projects	Actions	Processes	Supporting Technologies
Connection	Develop strategic alliances Create external partnerships Join a cooperative Partner with other departments Partner with other libraries	Community forums or town hall meetings Community fairs Online information sharing Conferences Staff meetings	Intranet forums E-mail folders Web conferences Conference calls Web pages or website Key web links
Contribution	Link contribution to performance Negotiate at least one group goal shared by all members Make contributions explicit among members Realign job functions	Build in check-in points to ensure contribution Create performance incentives and metrics Create group or team contract Find opportunities to showcase talent	360-degree feedback and peer reviews Stakeholder feedback E-mail folders Discussion forums for project information
Collaboration	Developed shared purpose and goals Define challenging problem to solve Explore innovative solutions	Put in place group or team design, e.g., subteams, core teams Develop pilot programs that showcase results	In-person meetings or face-to-face interactions Virtual meetings online Conference calls Groupware folders

■ conference calls, web pages, and web links that connect employees and constituents to information, vendors, and other stakeholders

You can find more examples of key actions, processes, and supporting technologies for contribution and collaboration in figure 7.5.

In the Integrated Applications Matrix Example (figure 7.6), we start with a specific strategic initiative, Strengthening Community Outreach, in its start-up or initial-stage activities, with the related subgoal of Developing a Community Database. In the matrix we list potential actions, processes, and supporting technologies that can be put into place to make the project successful. When you work through the chart, we recommend listing the top three to five items in each category that are the most critical to success. It is also suggested that you list the success criteria and top goals for your project or strategic initiative. This helps to provide clarity and guides your thinking so that you can focus on the most important actions, processes, and supporting technologies. The matrix worksheet can be used as a tool for any strategic initiative, project, or goal. We have included a blank worksheet (figure 7.7) so you can use it for your own library projects. We encourage you to use these worksheet tools as road maps for how to apply connection, contribution, and collaboration in your workplace.

The actions and leadership tools suggested in this section are meant to be used as your road map for action and results. Each tool is intended to help you jump-start library initiatives while developing the necessary personal and organizational leadership competencies required to "get the work done." Getting off to a successful start—or even getting to the point of starting—is particularly important in achieving success and creating sustainable change. The next section offers a few words of wisdom—we call them tips and tricks—for making a smoother transition to integrated leadership.

FIGURE 7.6   Integrated Applications Matrix—Example

Strategic Initiative: <u>Strengthen Community Outreach</u>

Application: Develop Community Database—Initial Stage Activities	**Actions**	**Processes**	**Supporting Technologies**
Connection	Meet with youth Meet with schools	Set up community forum for input	Face-to-face meetings Web templates for gathering input
Contribution	Enlist community members to be on project group Create shared goal endorsed by members	Do stakeholder analysis to identify talent needed both internally and in the community Identify talent gaps	Peer recommendations Online discussion folders
Collaboration	Create shared goals and vision Define challenges, e.g., budget, content development, maintenance	Organize vision and goal setting meeting Enlist key members to be on different project subteams	Conference calls Virtual meetings Project forum on the web-site

FIGURE 7.7   Integrated Applications Matrix Worksheet

Project/Initiative: _____

Application:	Actions	Processes	Supporting Technologies
Connection			
Contribution			
Collaboration			

Tips and Tricks for Making a Smooth Transition

In addition to the integration worksheets, we also offer a few well-proven tips and tricks for making a smooth transition as you do more connecting, contributing, and collaborating in your workplace.

1. Start with small and visible steps to create small wins. Remember what Kotter (1996) says about how to do successful change—it's important to create small wins. Don't expect too much from yourself and others when you first start making the transition. Although leading from a basis of connection, contribution, and collaboration is described as intuitive and natural by many leaders, there is always that first leap or transition that can be a bit messy. Like anything new, it is always better to go easy and be kind to ourselves and others while we are in a steep learning curve. When you have completed the worksheets, list only one major development goal or area of improvement. Identify your starting point—connection, contribution, or collaboration—and work from there. From that point you can gradually integrate your leadership actions and build your leadership competency or that of your library organization.

2. Focus on doing one or two things well. Once you gain some experience and momentum, move on to the next one or two things you want to change. Staff, stakeholders, and constituents will all respond more positively to one or two major successes than to minor or limited success across four or five initiatives. By focusing on doing one or two things well at the outset, you will also be able to create small wins and momentum for future actions. This is especially critical in the middle stages of a project or initiative, when you encounter difficulties that tend to slow down the process and lead to people questioning the project's benefits. Use the worksheets during different phases of a project or initiative to be sure you are on the right path. Make the necessary adjustments as you go.

3. Go slow to go fast. This is the new project maxim that we now apply on most of our project and consulting work with clients. When you base your leadership actions and results on connection, contribution, and collaboration, you may experience the process as going slower than if you were making decisions on your own or working in a small group of two to three people. If you go fast at the front end of the project and don't take the time to discuss how the group can do more connecting and partnering, identify each person's contributions and figure out what other talents are needed, gain consensus, and work through your collaboration process, then the group's communication and morale will begin to break down as the project progresses. You are also likely to begin to miss critical deadlines (these are often symptoms of going too fast). You end up going fast to go slow, not exactly what you want from a critical project. Rather than being displeased or impatient with "going slow to go fast," learn to use this process as a tactical tool.

4. Focus on group-based work that is cross-functional. The goal here is to (a) build the organizational capacity for the library staff to break down barriers that are created by "silos" or departments and (b) create an environment where people are more comfortable and proficient at connecting and collaborating.

Using group-based work projects as a way of applying connection, contribution, and collaboration builds success faster by engaging staff in the process and encouraging them to develop their own leadership capacities. It can be a trial-by-fire experience, yet if people are introduced to these leadership actions they at least have a frame of reference from which to take appropriate actions.

In this chapter we illustrated how to take each of the three leadership actions and integrate them from both a personal and an organizational perspective. Our application in action demonstrated what it can look like when you successfully integrate each of the different actions. So far we have presented key frameworks and tools and have illustrated the many applications of leadership. But any framework or tool has limitations, or what we like to call "sticky issues," that challenge us both practically and conceptually. In the next chapter we highlight some of these sticky issues and discuss how to handle them in real work situations.

8

Sticky Issues along the Way

Persistence often pays, but it requires an extra willingness to stay a rocky path when you have persuaded those above you and below you to embrace the course. —Useem 2001

In this chapter we will highlight some of the sticky problems that often arise in the process of implementing new or different leadership behaviors in the workplace. We suggest a few rules of the road that can help you keep a positive perspective on change, and we offer some suggestions for dealing with such sticky issues as influencing when you are not the boss, dealing with resistance to change, and creating shared accountability and responsibility.

General Rules of the Road

When we work with libraries on projects or initiatives that require some degree of change in the library system—it can be a process, technology, policy, or people-related—we always approach it with the following rules in mind. These rules help us to remember that change can be a positive and effective force when we understand and work with it on its own terms.

Rule One:
Lead with the Four Change Principles

We always refresh our memories by starting with the four change principles—organizing around change, doing the work that needs to be done, relying on the group as the primary unit of work, and sharing information. (See figure 8.1.)

FIGURE 8.1 The Four Change Principles

Change Principle	Complexity	Command and Control
Principle 1	Organizing around change	Organizing around control
Principle 2	Doing the work that needs to be done	Doing the work specified by job function
Principle 3	Relying on the group as the primary unit of work	Relying on the individual hero as the unit of work
Principle 4	Sharing information	Controlling information

When we approach a project, we do an initial diagnosis or problem-solving analysis. Based on the description of the problem, issue, or opportunity, which of the four change principles can we apply that would assist us in better understanding the problem, issue, or opportunity, and which one(s) might be a good first step toward resolution? For example, if you were implementing a new web reference and customer service in your library operations, you can take the web project and reflect on the following questions and considerations.

1. Are our library technology systems flexible or inflexible? Do our policies, which were developed and applied under a non-web operation, need to be changed to accommodate a web-based environment? Are our systems and processes designed to control and maintain our existing operation? Do we need to step back and add more flexibility so that we can organize around change? Any time you face a large-scale process- or systems-oriented change, the first change principle—organize around change—is a good one to keep at the top of your list.

2. Will the change require new skills? Do I need to cross-train? Do we need to create different performance criteria and incentives? Do the skills needed to be successful in the web extensions require skills building across the library, or just within one or two departments? In other words, how large-scale is the change? Perhaps your web automation project is an update or addition to an already developed web infrastructure and your goal is to extend this capability to new customers and markets. Upon further diagnosis, you realize that this next level of change or web expansion will require changes in staff functions and job responsibilities. In this case, you will want to focus on moving and shaping the organization in ways where your human resources can be flexible and adaptable and be focused on the work that needs to be done. In other words, you need to train staff, hire expertise to fill gaps, and enhance a customer service mind-set, so you start the project with the second change principle—doing the work that needs to be done.

3. Sometimes there are secondary impacts when you initiate a new project, especially when people have to change their routines, habits, and behaviors in order to make the change successful. This often becomes apparent when people,

with all good intentions, begin to work on a project but apply the "old" behaviors. In a sense, people have not yet "caught up" with the new routines and behaviors that the project demands, and so for a time, especially in the early and middle stages of a project, people lag the project. The third change principle—rely on the group as the primary unit of work—is always at play when people work at an individual level and the new project or challenge demands a more collaborative or group approach. Watch for this phenomenon in people's actions and behaviors. Anticipate the potential problem by instilling and supporting a group approach.

4. Always, always share information. This is one of the most important success criteria for any project or initiative. Trust people to use the information wisely. Train them to read and understand the project budget. Help them to understand the trade-offs so that the group can self-manage. If you are controlling information instead of sharing information, then you are micromanaging the project. This causes project delays and builds mistrust within the group and staff. Remember that it is especially important to share information when you are engaging in a new initiative because everyone is learning the new technology or process and needs as much information as possible to be effective quickly. Going back to our example, share the web extension budget, provide training manuals, and hold open discussions on potential processes that need to be updated or revised to meet the project goals.

These four change principles are always a good place to start because they can serve as an anchor for your approach. They help to keep you on course by reminding you of the connective and collaborative approach to leading change.

Rule Two:
Embrace the Messy Side of Collaboration

As mentioned in chapter 6, collaboration can be messy because it involves people grappling with problems, issues, or opportunities that are new, unknown, complex, and challenging. The collaborative process is a creative one; the answers and outcomes are never known or predetermined at the outset. People have to take in new information, unlearn old or outdated information, gain new knowledge, and learn to work differently with one another. If you expect precision, efficiency, and quick results early on, then you will be disappointed. Typically we start applying pressure to the project group by asking lots of questions too early in the process, wanting a review of the project timeline and needing a more firm budget. We like to "nail down" those details before the group is ready. This brings up what we describe as the "messy tension" in the collaborative process. There is usually an inherent tension between the needs of the leadership, who want to know more and feel confident about the progress of the project, and the pace of the group, which takes a much longer time to generate confidence and can never provide accurate details early enough.

Managing this tension effectively is a key role of the leader and the group members. Set reasonable timelines that give enough room for the group to engage in its early learning process yet provide enough evidence to leaders that the group is making progress. Set success criteria for the collaborative phases of a project. For example, one success criterion can be that key elements of the project will be mapped out in a format to determine customer service levels and costs. There are lots of good tips like these listed in chapter 6, especially on developing good processes for collaboration. Again, the key message here is to know at the outset that collaboration is inherently a messy process, and therefore you may need to readjust your expectations of success or look for evidence of progress in nontraditional ways. This will save you time and frustration.

Rule Three:
Learn to Say No: The Importance of Not Doing Too Much

This is a reminder of our tendency to try to do too much. Be aware of grand visions and project feature or scope "creep" by resisting the urge to ask too much of people. There is a difference between setting a "stretch" goal that takes into account both existing capabilities and future vision and an overly ambitious plan that may be desirable but is not achievable in the allotted time frame. Learning to say no is a critical leadership skill in today's work environment where people feel stretched too thin and resources are scarce. Be reasonable about workload and outcomes.

As the saying goes, it is always better to underpromise and overdeliver than to face the uphill battle of taking on too much at once with inadequate resources. As a leader, you need to watch for this and create reasonable expectations around behavior changes. Don't underestimate what it takes to change. Doing some of the worksheets in this book probably gave you an insight into how much change you can really take on at once. Remember to be kind to yourself and those around you. Appreciate the positive steps people take, even if they seem slow and not enough.

Rule Four:
Don't Blame the Person When It's Really the System

Sometimes we look around and wonder why our project is stalled or slowed. Our vendor is starting to backtrack on promised services, the city council has reduced our budget, and one of our agency partners is falling behind on their promised delivery. Do we look to the project manager for full accountability and responsibility? Do we look at the team members and wonder if we have the right people on the job? Do we have some of our best people on the project but things are still not coming together? If so, step back and ask yourself the following questions:

1. Are there existing processes, such as cross-department communications, that might be getting in the way of people's abilities to get the job done?

2. Do we have structures, such as compensation, that might be demotivating or preventing people from doing their best work?

3. Are there organizational norms around risk taking or decision making that are making it difficult for people to make progress?

Whenever you have a situation where good people are hindered in their efforts, it is often because the "system"—existing processes, structures, and norms—is getting in the way. A key leadership skill is to recognize that the problems often lie in the system and not with the group or the individual. Be careful not to attribute organizational roadblocks to an individual's performance. Granted, a good project manager needs to be able to recognize and work around or change roadblocks. But even the best project managers and high-performing work groups need leadership to make system-level changes that are usually outside the authority of the project group yet stand as barriers to progress. Focus your efforts on removing system-level roadblocks so employees can make a meaningful contribution.

With these rules in mind, let's turn our attention to some sticky issues we are likely to face along the way.

Navigating through Sticky Issues

"Sticky issues" is a term we use to describe the less glamorous yet ever-present aspects of leading with connection, contribution, and collaboration. As we move through our processes and engage in our daily work life, change and complexity are always present. When we are always in change and flux, we crave stability and a break from the chaos and uncertainty of our situation. Yet these are leadership and life skills that we have to develop if we are to find meaning, reward, and satisfaction within ourselves and our workplace. In our interviews with library, industry, and government leaders at all levels of management, we discovered three of the stickiest issues when it comes to leading effective change. They are:

1. How to influence when you are not the boss
2. What to do when your boss is command and control
3. How to work with resistance to change

How to Influence When You Are Not the Boss

This is one of the most common questions we get from all levels of managers and leaders who want to get things done yet feel they lack the authority and positional power or title to make changes. An excellent resource on this topic is a book by Geoffrey Bellman called *Getting Things Done When You Are Not in Charge* (2001). He reminds us that "we succeed by helping others succeed; our accomplishment is dependent on theirs" (Bellman 2001, 1). Many of us grow up with the expectation that someone is in charge when really this is an illusion; the real contradiction is our disappointment that someone isn't in charge and that each of us has to take charge. As a result, we often look to others when in fact the answer lies in our own capacity to take action on behalf of ourselves and those around us. If we begin to understand that no one is really in charge and that we are all responsible for taking action, we can begin to engage in work differently and understand that we are better off influencing than we are trying to "be in charge" and "be the boss." Remember, even bosses complain that they are not in charge (Bellman 2001).

Bellman offers a framework that we find practical, effective, and inspirational. Influencing others happens when our desires or "wants," as Bellman calls them, are aligned with other people's and the organization's "wants." Once we assess the organizational and political reality, we can begin to take positive action and influence others. Here again, we influence others positively by taking actions that move our individual "wants" into alignment with other people's and the organization's "wants."

Along with Bellman, we offer a few helpful guidelines.

1. Build common understanding and a shared appreciation for everyone's wants throughout the organization. In chapter 5 on contribution, we suggested you check in with group members by asking them what their contribution is to the project. Repeat this same check-in process and modify it by asking each person about their wants (in addition to their contributions). Spend time talking to colleagues, key partners, and stakeholders one-on-one to find out about each person's wants. Use the information to build a common understanding and platform for taking action that is in alignment with wants and needs.

2. Face the politics and aim to build a positive political climate by dealing with people face-to-face, finding shared wants, taking the larger or longer view (over the short-term gain), using openness to counter secrets, increasing your tolerance for ambiguity, and being willing to understand others while reminding yourself that understanding does not mean agreement (Bellman 2001, 51). In other words, have a realistic assessment of the library's politics and work with what you have to begin to make gains.

3. One of the most important things you can do is to seek to work in concert with the priorities of the library. Be sure your actions and time are linked to these priorities in concrete ways. Once you link or connect your actions to the top priorities, people will pay more attention to you because they know that your "wants" are aligned with the organization's "wants" or priorities. This is another effective way to influence and have a voice. We also support Bellman's advice to follow the money as a way of knowing where the project priorities are in your organization. Know what projects are funded, what initiatives are being considered, and where the budget funds go. Be involved in projects and activities that are funded—go where the action is by following the money!

4. Spend time building relationships with partners, key stakeholders, and decision makers inside and outside your organization. Ask for a review of your project plan or advice on a key next step; any way to get feedback from others in order to build relationships along the way. We use the term "socialize," meaning to talk to many different people and constituents about an idea and hence "socialize" it, especially when you are first formulating an idea and want to both build support and avoid pitfalls along the way.

5. Remember that leadership, like nature, abhors a vacuum! Take risks and have the courage to just jump in and take initiative. It's an amazing feeling to know that others will follow if you act with conviction and in the service of the needs of everyone around you.

What to Do When Your Boss Is Command and Control

We get asked this question all the time when we do our workshops. It seems that people collectively believe that if only their bosses weren't so command and control, many of their problems would go away or be easily resolved. So how do you work effectively with what you may perceive as command and control bosses? An excellent resource on this topic is a book by Michael Useem, *Leading Up: How to Lead Your Boss so You Both Win* (2001). We like Useem's framework because, like Bellman, it offers a philosophy of partnership and mutual gains as a way to get results and lead effectively. Connecting, contributing, and collaborating are all leadership actions that assume a solid foundation of partnering, and so a leadership skill set must include "leading up" or "coaching up."

One piece of advice: if you believe that your boss is leading from a command and control approach and you are leading from a connecting and collaborating approach, you should at least review some of your own leadership behaviors to make sure that they are indeed differing approaches. Sometimes managers rail at command and control bosses and then turn around and repeat the same behavior in their project or staff meetings. We only say this to remind everyone that after decades of command and control leadership, it does take time to truly lead in a different way. So here are a few words of wisdom on how to deal with command and control bosses.

1. Always start with your self. Change starts at home. Since it is difficult to change others, start by changing yourself. Become aware and conscious of your own leadership actions around connection, contribution, and collaboration.

2. Model the way. People will come around and respond amazingly fast when you put into practice what you desire from others.

3. Work with what you have first. If it is difficult for you to influence your boss, then at least start within your own staff or project team. Start where you do have influence and power and make changes. You don't need to scale the mountain on the first day. Take some good steps and establish a base camp. Then reassess and prepare to take your next steps.

4. In the meantime, schedule some time with your boss. Find out her top priorities and let her know she has your support. Useem (2001) offers some good advice in this area. To start with, inform your boss of any new events or actions that impact her top priorities. Show that you care about her initiatives and that you can be trusted with more information. Communicate on a regular basis and keep people in the loop. Don't assume they have information or know everything.

5. If you really disagree with a direction or want to offer a new direction, build your case. Anecdotal stories are interesting but you need facts. Present a good case for change with the goal of generating enough interest to warrant a

more widespread conversation (at the executive, board, or city/county government level), and offer suggestions for doable action steps. Show that you understand the implications of the proposed change on the organization's people, processes, technologies, customers, and budget.

6. Don't wait for your boss to "take charge." Go out and take responsible action yourself. When we talk with senior-level leaders, their biggest complaint is that first-time and middle-level managers wait for approval before taking action. Senior leaders want people in the organization to take responsibility. You might be caught in the loop of feeling like you work for a command and control boss when, in fact, she is just waiting for you to do something and act like a leader.

7. It is better to ask for forgiveness than permission. No project or strategic initiative is without controversy and risk. Don't wait until everyone likes your idea. Work really hard to get the majority to like it and then move from there. Sometimes it's just easier to do the right thing and ask for forgiveness later. This philosophy works well if you are effective and have a good track record for success, so use the leverage you have and take advantage of opportunities that come your way. Again, even if your boss is not so supportive at the outset, she will come around if your actions are in alignment with her priorities.

How to Work with Resistance to Change

Resistance always accompanies any change effort or project. Although we generally view resistance as undesirable, it is becoming clear to us that resistance is good and needs to be embraced if the project or organization wants to move forward. A great source of insight and information on this topic is Rick Maurer's book *Beyond the Wall of Resistance* (1996). Maurer lists the following four primary values of working with resistance.

1. Using the force of resistance can increase our success rate and speed the time it takes to implement a new idea. Typical forms of resistance are silence, confusion, immediate criticism, denial (that change needs to happen), malicious compliance (people comply early on and appear supportive yet drag their feet), sabotage (people literally doing all they can to stop the idea from gaining ground or proceeding), and easy agreement (people all nod their heads in agreement at first, but later on in the change process, they realize the implications and begin to engage in active resistance). Become aware of the signs of resistance and be able to work with them at the individual and group level. Usually resistance in these forms means that people have deep reservations about the idea and are fearful of the change it implies. Pay attention to how people both think and feel about the change. If you do this up front, then there will be less resistance in the later stages of the project.

2. Showing respect toward those who resist change builds stronger relationships, not only improving the change at hand but providing a solid base for future changes. Here we want to honor those who seem resistant to the idea. Oftentimes people want more facts and a bridge or road map on how to move from today into tomorrow. They need more information before they can support

the change. This will help you to slow down and put processes into place that acknowledge resistance and assist people in working through their own fears and concerns. Remember, you yourself have resistance, so acknowledge your own feelings and fears. It's healthier to get it out than to let it undermine your convictions and actions.

3. Working with resistance increases the likelihood that all parties can meet at least some of their goals. When resistance is open and on the table, each of us has the opportunity to voice not only our concerns but also our visions and wants. Being open enables us to have honest conversations that lead to collaborative problem solving. Being open also keeps us in connection with each other and builds strong relationships. These are all positive outcomes of resistance to change.

4. The voice of resistance can keep us from taking untimely or foolish actions. Sometimes we think we have a great idea and then proceed to action, maybe too quickly. Resistance can be extremely helpful in flushing out ideas that need further examination, anticipating pitfalls or roadblocks, and identifying resources or capabilities that we need to have in order to be successful. We always try to find the naysayer in the group and start with that person. Usually if we can work with resistance at the deepest levels, the change has a realistic chance for success.

The message here is clear. Look for resistance to change: identify it, honor it, embrace it, and work with it.

Learning from You

So you've read the rules of the road and learned some of the sticky issues that confront us when we lead our libraries in this time of change and complexity. We invite you to contact us with your stories and examples of how you have used the leadership practices in this book. Like you, we are always learning more about leading based on connection, contribution, and collaboration. We want to know the many creative and engaging ways you have taken these ideas and actions and applied them in your library workplace. We are always interested in the results—both successes and key lessons learned. If you have questions, want to tell us your stories, or otherwise dialogue with us, write to us at The Olson Group, Inc., 11420 Tower Hill Road, Nevada City, CA 95959, or e-mail us at Christi.olson@ mindspring.com.

Epilogue

The Future Is Already Here

*Grace has success. In small matters it
is favorable to undertake something.*
— *The I Ching (Book of Changes)*

We started this book by talking about the challenges libraries are facing: dealing with rapid technological and market change, building the competencies of next-generation leaders, managing a diversity of customers, adjusting to rapidly changing demographics in our communities, and making do with what seems like fewer resources. The work ahead is more of the same. More than likely, we are at the beginning of this curve and we can expect both surprises and challenges in the next twenty-five years.

The library of the future is already here. Digital content is now the content of choice, online service and web infrastructure are rapidly becoming the new virtual library, and our physical libraries are multiuse and much more open, with a blend of community and commercial interests. Money is shifting away from traditional library functions and into digital content and supporting services (Stratigos and Strouse 2003). Indeed, libraries are becoming a 24-7 operation with anywhere/anytime access. Specialized libraries, corporate libraries, and smaller public libraries have the capacity to be on more equal footing with large urban public libraries because everyone, large and small, has the capability to log on and subscribe to the same digital content. Private collections of digital content, like those of Bill Gates, will surpass those of many large libraries. It's a world of mass media, digital content, no geographic boundaries, just-in-time information, specialized customer groups, and global access.

So what is the role of library leaders? We say their role is to lead in this time of great transition and opportunity. Stratigos and Strouse write that the information professional has to become a trusted adviser and consultant. The librarian is the gateway to information and not a gatekeeper. It takes a "do with" rather than a "do for" philosophy to stay competitive in today's environment (Stratigos and Strouse 2003). Physical libraries are becoming collaborative spaces. Major urban libraries like those in Salt Lake City, Portland, Phoenix, Baltimore, and San Francisco are examples of this new digital collaborative space. The role of the librarian and the function of the library are undergoing radical change. It is happening to a lesser or greater degree to everyone involved with libraries and content and information management and access.

This major transition of libraries in the digital age requires leadership skills and competencies that are much more in alignment with the larger customer and technology trends and market forces. Connection, contribution, and collaboration are the skills you need to bridge the gap between today's leadership competencies and tomorrow's vision. Our goal is to have these leadership practices become an essential part of your toolkit as you create and take action on your own road map. We want these leadership practices to provide value and support to you in your leadership goals as you continue to evolve and grow the libraries and leaders of the future. The future is already here—let's be open to the challenges and discoveries that such transitions hold for us. Go with grace, and be sure to start by doing something. All success starts with action.

REFERENCES

Bellman, G. 2001. *Getting Things Done When You Are Not in Charge.* San Francisco: Berrett-Koehler.

Bryant, J., and K. Poustie. *Competencies Needed by Public Library Staff.* Gutersloh, Ger.: Bertelsmann Foundation, 2001.

Cooperrider, D. L., and D. Whitney. 1999. *Appreciative Inquiry.* San Francisco: Berrett-Koehler.

Holpp, L. 1999. *Managing Teams.* New York: McGraw-Hill.

Hout, T. M., and J. C. Carter. 1995. "Getting It Done: New Roles for Senior Executives." *Harvard Business Review* (November-December).

Kotter, J. 1996. *Leading Change.* Boston: Harvard Business School Press.

Kouzes, J., and B. Posner. 1995. *The Leadership Challenge.* San Francisco: Jossey-Bass.

Laughlin, S. 2000. *Library Networks in the New Millennium: Top Ten Trends.* Chicago: American Library Association.

Maurer, R. 1996. *Beyond the Wall of Resistance.* Austin, Tex.: Bard Books.

Mayo, D., and J. Goodrich. 2002. *Staffing for Results: A Guide to Working Smarter.* Chicago: American Library Association.

Nelson, S. 2001. *The New Planning For Results: A Streamlined Approach.* Chicago: American Library Association.

Nelson, S., E. Altman, and D. Mayo. 2000. *Managing for Results: Effective Resource Allocation for Public Libraries.* Chicago: American Library Association.

Schrage, M. 1995. *No More Teams: Mastering the Dynamics of Collaboration.* New York: Currency Doubleday.

Singer, P. 2002. *Developing a Compensation Plan for Your Library.* Chicago: American Library Association.

Stratigos, A., and R. Strouse. 2003. "Library of the Future." *Online Magazine,* January-February, at www.onlinemag.net.

Useem, M. 2001. *Leading Up: How to Lead Your Boss so You Both Win.* New York: Three Rivers.

Wheatley, M. 2001. *Leadership and the New Science: Discovering Order in a Chaotic World.* 2d ed. San Francisco: Berrett-Koehler.

Wilhelm, R., and Cary F. Baynes, trans. 1950. *The I Ching or Book of Changes.* Princeton, N.J.: Princeton University Press.

INDEX

Christi A. Olson is a managing partner in The Olson Group, Inc., a consulting firm specializing in leadership and change management. She is also an associate dean at the Fielding Graduate Institute in Organization Development and Management. Olson has over twenty years' experience in senior leadership. She has worked with clients in business, nonprofit organizations, education, and government, and she is a frequent speaker at conferences and conducts workshops on leadership and change.

Paula M. Singer is president of The Singer Group, Inc., a consulting firm in Baltimore that specializes in compensation, human resources, and organization development. She was formerly executive director of the Classified Municipal Employees Association of Baltimore, a labor organization representing 6,000 municipal employees. Singer also teaches graduate-level classes in organization development and human resources at Johns Hopkins University, Baltimore. She is the author of *Developing a Compensation Plan for Your Library* (2002) and coauthor of *Best Practices in Learning and Development* (2002).